The Care and Repair of Small Marine Diesels

Chris Thompson

The Care and Repair of Small Marine Diesels

ADLARD COLES NAUTICAL
London

Published by Adlard Coles Nautical
an imprint of A & C Black (Publishers) Ltd
35 Bedford Row, London WC1R 4JH

First published in 1982 by Adlard Coles
Reprinted with amendments 1983
Reprinted 1984
Reprinted in paperback 1987, 1988, 1989, 1990,
1991, 1996

ISBN 0-7136

A CIP catalogue record for this book is available from the British Library.

Printed and bound in Great Britain by
Hartnolls Ltd, Bodmin, Cornwall.

Contents

List of Illustrations

Acknowledgements

The author gratefully acknowledges the assistance of the following companies, in particular staff and one-time colleagues at Perkins Engines Ltd, in providing drawings or photographs and other data used in this book; without this willing help the task of preparing much of the material would have proved more onerous.

Motorfabriken Bukh A/S, Kalundborg.
Carl Hurth Maschinen-und Zahnradfabrik, Munich.
R. A. Lister and Company Ltd.
Lucas-CAV Ltd.
Mermaid Marine Engines Ltd.
Petters Limited.
Perkins Engines Ltd.
Stuart Turner Limited.
TI-Dieseltune Ltd.
A. N. Wallis & Co. Ltd.
Watermota Ltd.

Preface

If on reading through this book you feel that you have learned something about engines in general and small marine diesels in particular, I shall be satisfied; if, more importantly, you have gained some better understanding of the machinery of your boat and improved your own ability to see that it works efficiently over a long life without failing, then my purpose will have been served.

Mechanical problems are almost always the result of some human weakness or deficiency. Before you put to sea, my advice is to get hold of the engine manufacturer's instruction book for your particular model and read it so that you know what is in it and where to find it. I cannot hope to explain all, nor indeed to give detailed information on every model of every make of engine, although descriptions of some well-known and typical makes are given as a guide. The book's main purpose will have been achieved if after reading it you feel you have improved your understanding, improved your ability, and gained confidence in dealing with your motor. After all, somebody's life, if not your own, may well depend on it.

one

Background

The adoption and growth of heavy oil engines as an alternative to steam power dates back just over a hundred years. After Doctor Rudolf Diesel's patents were taken out in 1892, development was first confined to stationary engines which were large and heavy by today's standards. The turn of the century saw a rapid application of the diesel in the field of marine engines, although they were still formidable pieces of machinery. Their main attraction when compared with existing steam engines was the absence of the need for boilers, coupled with convenience and economy in the use of fuel.

The development of early submarines (1910) was very much dependent on the availability of diesel engines, the so-called lightweight engine range built by MAN in Germany being of the two-stroke variety and developing, according to the number of cylinders, between 150 hp and 1,200 hp; these engines ran at maximun speeds of between 400 and 500 rpm, and their weight to power ratio was about 35 lb per hp. This compares with a ratio of approximately 10 lb per hp for some present-day engines for boats.

The need to repair engines at sea is associated with the bigger engine and does not concern us here, but it is mentioned because, up to recent years, the way most small marine diesels were constructed followed the lines of big ships' propulsion units. This is one of the reasons why diesels have the reputation for being heavy and rugged (Fig 1). They were costly to build because so much iron went into their construction, their design did not lend itself to quantity production and they tended to be made in relatively small numbers. If they were reliable it was almost entirely due to the absence of electric ignition. The tendency today is to use better materials and more sophisticated manufacturing methods to achieve a more compact and lighter design without any sacrifice of life or reliability.

Development

The extensive growth in the number of diesel engines for small boats and yachts has been made possible by the parallel development of cars and light trucks. The growth thus owes as much to the automotive industry as to the heavy marine engineering industry, if not more. The technologies of each industry have blended to produce the lightweight, high speed marine diesel of today. Inherited first were the traditional standards of reliability and fuel economy of the big diesels, second were the quantity production techniques coupled with the newer materials of the automotive industry.

Development was accelerated during the years 1939–1945. This was the period of World War II which saw so many advances in technology in response to unprecedented demands. One of these was for lightweight diesels for small high-speed craft for use in coastal operations (Fig 2). Not unnaturally the conclusion of hostilities saw many hun-

Fig 1. A marine diesel of 1927. Petter two cylinder two stroke of 20 b.h.p.

dreds of these boats and their engines surplus to military requirements, and they eventually found their way into the commercial and pleasure boat markets (Fig 3).

Since that date the development of lightweight diesels has progressed to embrace high-powered turbocharged engines of over 300 shp right down to 6 hp single cylinder units, so that most small craft inboard engines made are now diesels, with the exception of some sports and racing craft and amateur conversions of car engines. The problems of worldwide availability of fuels are unlikely to alter this pattern in the foreseeable future, but in situations of shortage it is likely that the economy of the diesel will always weigh substantially on its side against possible alternatives (Figs 4 and 5).

Why has the diesel engine become supreme as a power unit in marine craft? Putting accidents of history apart, it is because it

Fig 2. A World War II 60′ pinnace operated by the R.A.F.

Fig 3. The Perkins S6M 6 cylinder engine developing 120 b.h.p. at 2200 revs. min. Three of these power units were installed in the pinnace illustrated in Fig 2.

offers to the boat owner these inherent advantages over anything else available:

Reliability
Simplicity
Economy in the use of available fuels
Minimal fire risk
Relatively long life

The foregoing brief historical resumé is intended to show something of the background behind your engine and to give you, the boat owner, some confidence in it as your power unit, something in which you can put your trust when your life is at stake. Always remember, though, that for a safe passage it is not the machinery but the human element

Fig 4. An example of present day small engines. The Petter AC2M unit of 12 b.h.p.

which is the most important, and that includes not only the ability to do the right thing in a crisis, but diligence in having taken steps beforehand in getting to understand and take care of your boat, equipment, and motor.

First Principles

Many descriptions of the diesel engine rely on drawing comparisons with petrol engines, because so many people have a fairly good notion of the latter from their cars, and the engines look somewhat similar. This could be

Fig 5. An example of present day high powered engines. The Perkins T6.3544 developing 175 s.h.p. at 2600 revs. min.

a starting point to our diesel description, but apart from the fact that the petrol engine was historically first on the scene, as you will have gathered from my earlier remarks, the diesel of today is in no sense an adaption of the former, even if in a number of ways it is similar in construction. The diesel when it first saw the light of day was more a cousin of the reciprocating steam engine where, instead of burning coal in a boiler and using the steam in the engine cylinders, the inventor's idea was that coal was to be directly sprayed into the cylinder in finely powdered form and there, when combined with air, burned. Hence the term internal combustion engine. (Diesel's original patent did not specify the actual fuel to be used, but did specifically mention pulverised coal as one of the possibilities.)

One thing evident from the earliest days of

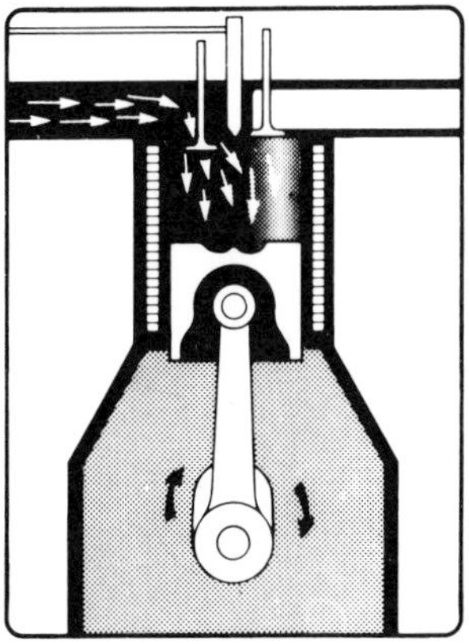

(a) Induction.

(c) Power or expansion.

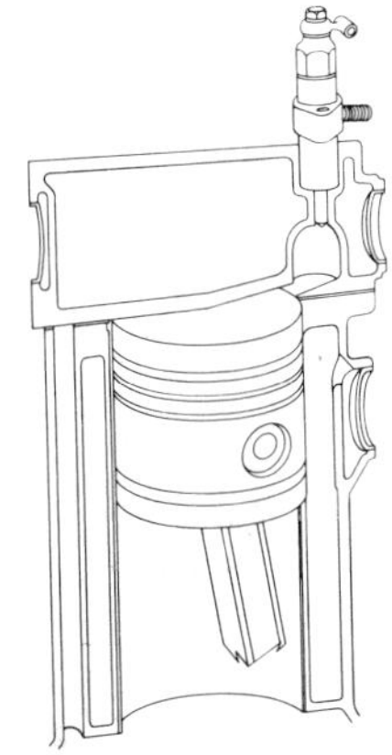

(e) Indirect injection.

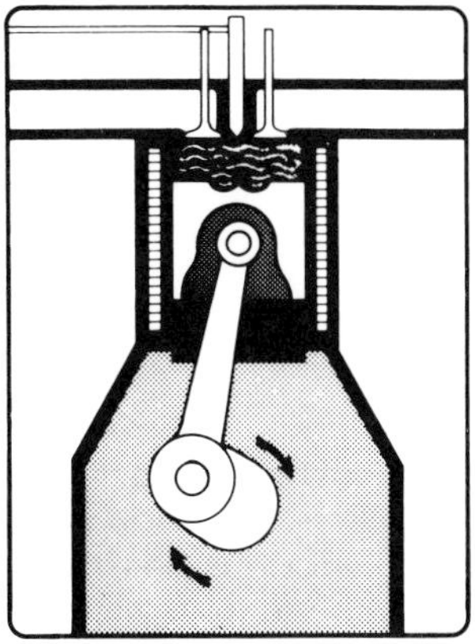

(b) Compression.

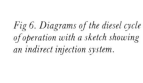

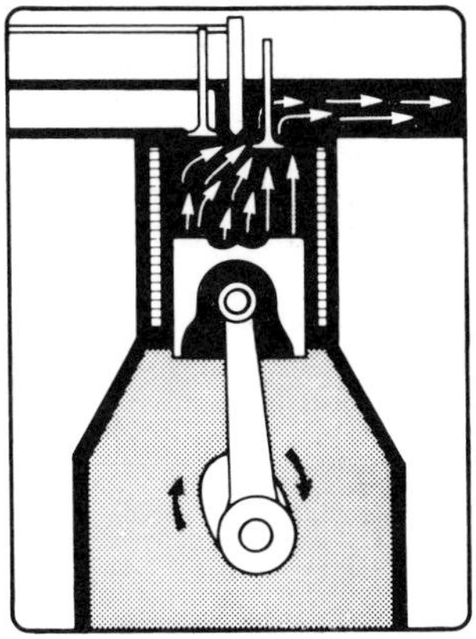

(d) Exhaust.

Fig 6. Diagrams of the diesel cycle of operation with a sketch showing an indirect injection system.

the diesel, and its subsequent development, is the absence of any form of outside ignition. This lack of dependence on electricity is one of the principal factors contributing to its superior reliability over most other forms of internal combustion engine. Sometimes

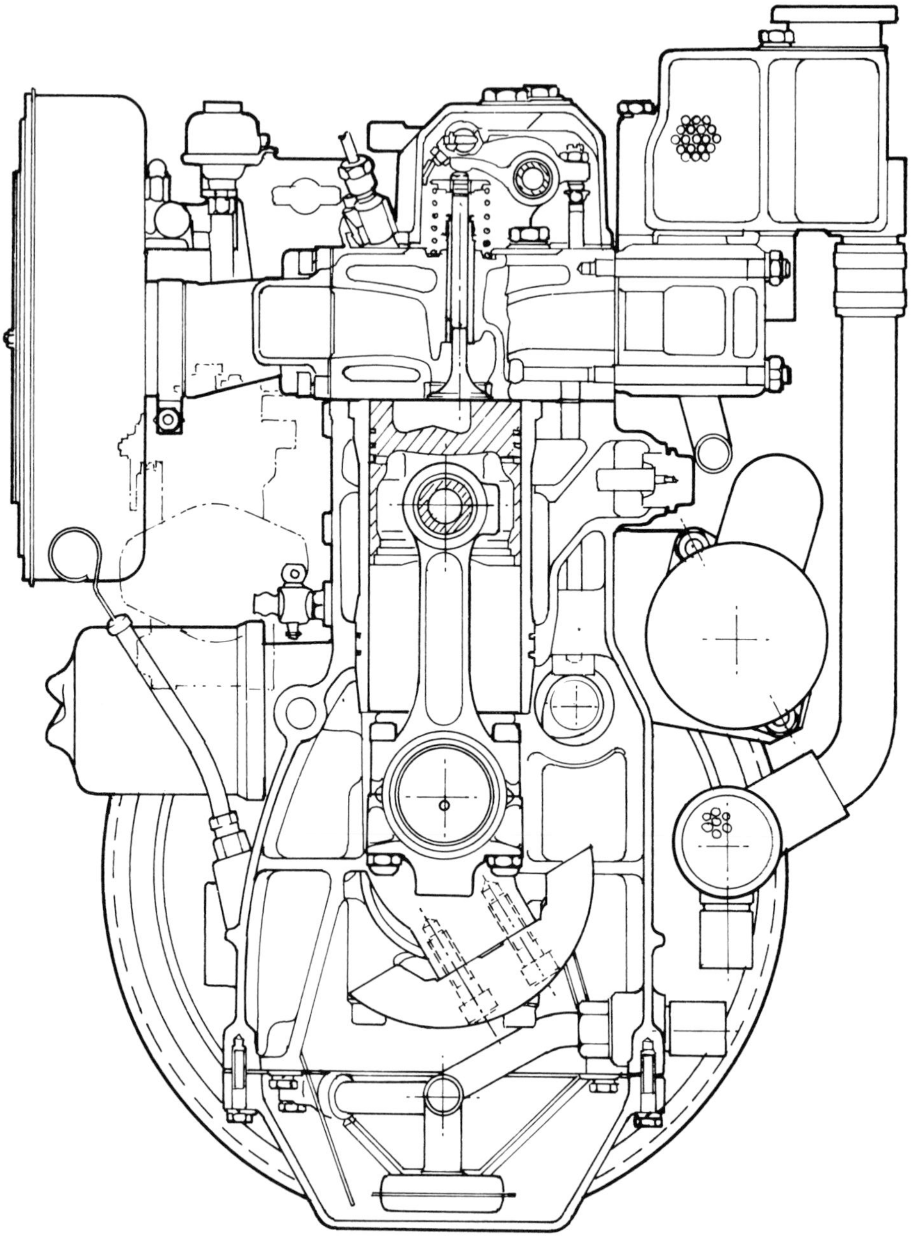

Fig 7. Cross sectional drawing of a Bukh three cylinder engine type OV36 showing many typical features of small marine diesels arranged for direct injection.

diesel engines were correctly described as compression ignition engines, a term which has since fallen into disuse.

The Diesel Cycle. Operation is illustrated diagrammatically in Fig 6(a)–(d), which depict the cycle of operation of a four-stroke engine. A diesel works on a fuel which is of low volatility and at ordinary temperatures non flammable. The oil is introduced directly into the cylinders in which atmospheric air has been drawn by the downgoing piston through the open inlet valve and then compressed as the piston rises (Figs 6a and b). In this process the air becomes very hot in much the same way that it does when you inflate a bicycle tyre with a hand pump. At a point near to the end of the compression stroke (b) fuel is injected through an atomiser (shown between the two valves) when it ignites immediately in the hot air without the need for a spark of any kind, finally burning completely as the piston moves down under the pressure of the gases above it (c).

Towards the end of the power or expansion stroke the exhaust valve opens and the spent gases are allowed to escape as the piston rises again (d), after which the process described is repeated. In a direct injection engine as shown the volume of air in the cylinder before the piston rises compared with the final compressed volume of air with the piston at the top of its travel is in the ratio of approximately 16 to 1. This is known as the compression ratio (C.R.). The combustion chamber is formed by a special shape in the piston crown.

In an indirect injection engine shown diagrammatically in Fig 6(e) the fuel is injected into a small chamber in the cylinder head in communication with the cylinder by a narrow passage. Indirect injection engines often have compression ratios of up to 21 to 1. Discussion of the relative merits of the two types of combustion chamber is somewhat outside the scope of the present book but the user may find that in cold starting the direct injection engine is a little easier, but the atomisers may require more frequent attention.

Engines operating on the two-stroke cycle exist but, with one notable exception, they are not now in general use as small boat engines and are usually restricted to big ships.

Construction

Most small marine diesels are similar in construction, but with individual differences. In a book of this size all cannot be described in detail, but in the next chapters illustrations are given of a few of the models which are manufactured today and used all over the world.

The basic construction of the small diesel consists first of a cast iron box, more or less rectangular in shape, enclosing the crankshaft, hence it is called the crankcase. One or more cylinders may be firmly attached by bolts to the crankcase, or in many designs may be cast integrally with it. Bolted to it underneath there is a pan or sump for holding lubricating oil and on top of the cylinders the cylinder heads are also bolted. Usually at the forward end of the crankcase are situated the gears driving the camshaft and other auxiliaries, and at the rear the drive is taken from the crankshaft through the transmission or reverse gear and clutch. The flywheel may be at either end.

two
Crankcase and Cylinder Block

The crankshaft and its main bearings are replaceable on overhaul, so there is nothing to wear out in the crankcase itself, which retains its identity and usually bears the maker's stamped serial number for the engine. When integral with the cylinder block casting, this contains the removable sleeves for each cylinder and these can be renewed if needed. The only things which can go wrong with the crankcase and cylinder block are, first, the face of the joint between it and the cylinder head; secondly, there may be frost damage, which is dealt with later under the heading of cooling systems.

Crankshafts

Crankshafts vary a good deal in design from engine to engine, more particularly in the smaller sizes of single or twin cylinder engines where methods of manufacture differ. For engines with three or more cylinders the main differences lie in whether or not they have integral or bolted-on weights, which are designed to provide some degree of counterbalance for the connecting rod and piston assemblies. The main points of difference which need concern us are in the method of attachment of the driven parts at each end, and the hardness of the crankpins and journals (Fig 8).

Whether the material of the shaft is special cast iron or forged alloy steel, it is common for the crankpins and main journals to have been given some treatment to increase their hardness and thus improve durability. Under reasonable conditions of service, therefore, crankshaft wear should be minimal, and regrinding may not be necessary before several thousands of hours of use. Unfortunately sand, dirt, water or other foreign matter seem to find their way into marine engines all too often and can do great harm to pistons, bearings and the rubbing surfaces of crankshafts, etc, so that it is not unusual to find crankshaft journals and crankpins scored or worn at earlier periods than one would expect from the number of hours run. The guide in repair must be the degree of ovality of the shaft, scoring of the shaft, scoring of the bearings, pitting in the bearing surfaces and actual wear of the latter. This is indicated first by visual examination showing polished marking, and finally confirmed by measurement (Fig 9).

The makers usually specify dimensions for checking the acceptable wear of these parts, but the owner does not normally have the means of taking these measurements nor the expertise to do so, and help from a friend who does is well worth having in this event (Fig 10); see chapter 14.

The decision in regard to using a reground crankshaft must be determined by circumstances. There are two main considerations. The first is whether undersized bearings are available and, if so, what degree of regrind will be necessary to remove the effects of scoring or wear in the shaft. The second is whether the reground shaft is up to

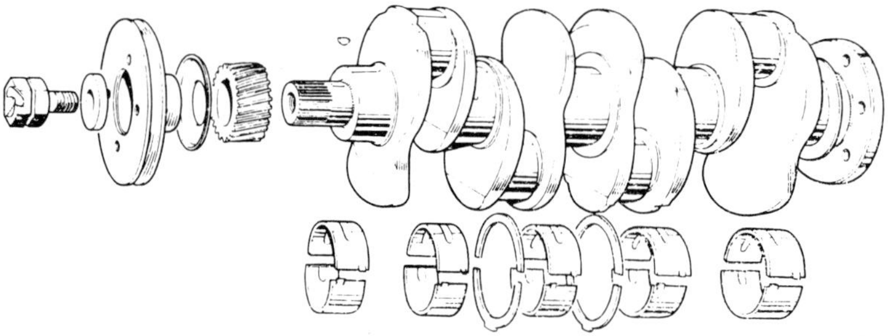

Fig 8. Crankshaft with integral balance weights. Strip type main bearing shells are also shown with thrust washers at the centre main journal to locate the shaft axially. Splines (serrations) are provided for front end attachments of timing gears and pulley, and a flange for the flywheel at the aft end.

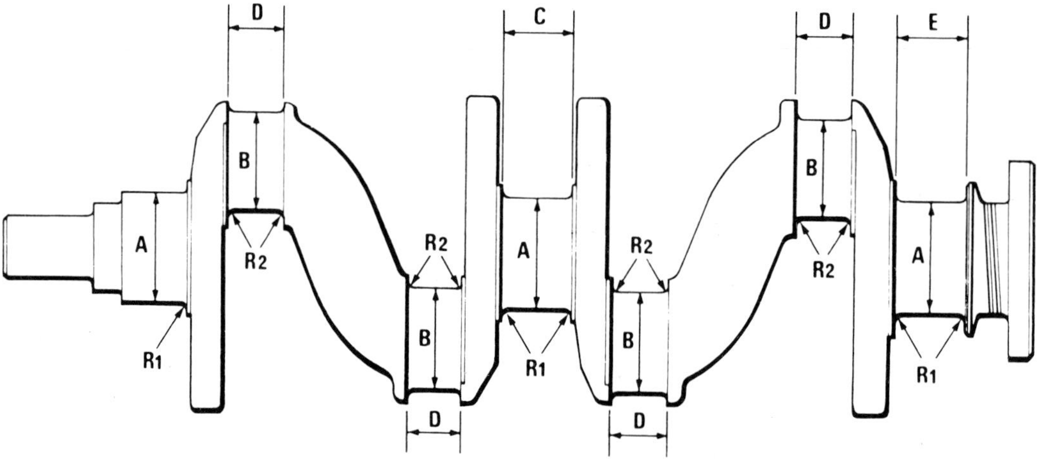

Fig 9. Diagram of typical 4 cylinder crankshaft showing dimensions which have to be checked on overhaul. In addition to the more obvious dimensions for diameters A and B, and widths C, D, E, the fillet radii R1 and R2 are most important.

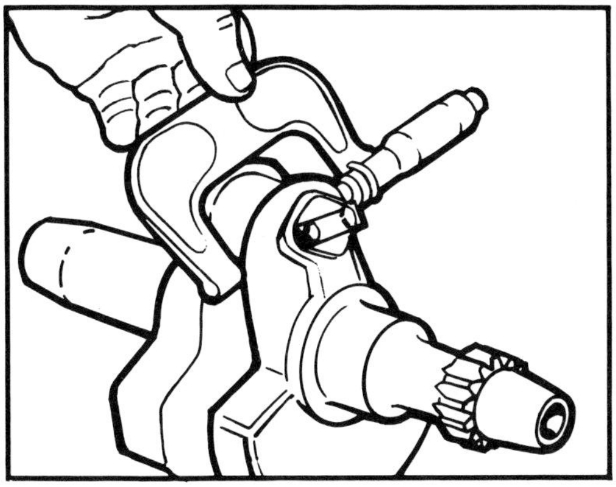

Fig 10. A single cylinder engine crankshaft (Stuart) showing micrometer measurement of crankpin diameter, and tapered end for flywheel fixing.

the maker's standard as to freedom from surface cracks, finish, straightness and correctness of fillet radius (see Fig 9). The importance of these features cannot be overemphasised when one reflects that, while the actual failure of crankshafts is a rare occurrence, where it has occurred the chances are two to one that is has been a shaft which has been incorrectly reground.

Associated Parts. We mentioned earlier the attachment at each end of the crank of the timing gears and of the flywheel. Where the latter is fitted on a taper, sometimes a trace of fretting is indicative of lack of tightness, and care should be exercised in refitting to ensure that the parts mate together properly; offer them up with engineers' marking blue, obtainable from tool stores, spread thinly on one part and checking the corresponding witness on the other. Where the contact is shown to be less than 75 per cent, the parts can usually be hand-lapped. After removing the key from the keyway, apply a smear of grinding paste to the mating surfaces, and reassemble the parts with the nut fingertight. Keeping the crank stationary, the flywheel is given half a turn each way by hand several times. Wash out the paste with solvent and re-check the fit as before. Repeat as required. Above all, make sure when they are finally bolted together that they are properly tightened to the correct torque, since no amount of locking devices will compensate for an undertorqued nut. Manufacturers specify their recommended figures for the more important fastenings: these require the use of a torque-measuring wrench when finally tightening up.

Flywheel

In the case of single- and twin-cylinder engines, the main function of the flywheel is to smooth out the firing impulses of the cylinders. In the case of engines having more than three cylinders, the need for a flywheel is not very great – it decreases inversely with the number of cylinders. The chief remaining purpose of the flywheel is to provide a fixing for the gear ring for starting purposes. With small engines not provided with electric starters, a heavy flywheel does assist in the hand-cranking process of getting the engine over compression, but there is a limit to the usefulness of weight of flywheel in achieving a satisfactory start. I once spent a week recovering from the effects of trying unsuccessfully to hand crank a large four cylinder diesel; the flywheel was so heavy and the frictional drag so great that four of us had difficulty in reaching the minimum speed necessary for igniting the fuel.

The Connecting Rod

Connecting the piston, with its up and down or reciprocating motion, to the crankshaft with its rotary motion is the connecting rod, with bearings at the points of connection. The connecting rod is almost always made from a steel forging or stamping (Fig 11). The smaller of the two bearings at the upper connection with the piston is called the small-end, and consists of a plain bush made in phosphor bronze material, or of steel lined with antifriction material, pre-finished and pressed into the connecting rod eye and running with a fine clearance on the gudgeon or piston pin. This bearing depends, in larger engines, on pressure lubrication from a hole drilled along the length of the rod, taking oil pressure from the big-end or crankpin bearings. Usually in smaller engines its lubrication depends on splash and mist only, thus

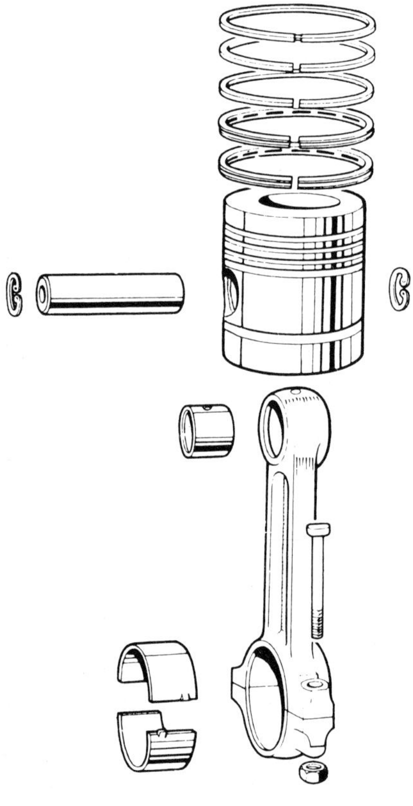

Fig 11. A piston, connecting rod and big-end bearing assembly.

obviating the need for providing the drilled hole in the rod, which would weaken it.

The small-end bearing does not normally call for any special attention between major overhauls and enjoys a trouble-free life. It is hard to measure for wear, which usually occurs locally in the bottom half of the bush only, but it may become pitted if for any reason sea water has entered the lubrication system. On major overhaul it is best replaced (Fig 12).

Bearings. The big-end or connecting rod bearing on the other hand may well be a limiting factor in the overhaul life of the engine. That is to say, wear of the big-end bearings may determine when the engine must be taken out of the boat and opened up, and if necessary completely overhauled. Manufacturers have different criteria when designing engines, and of course levels of performance and efficiency are principal factors. Other considerations are those of cost and ease of manufacture and also, not necessarily last in importance, are reliability and overhaul life. I mention these things because, apart from sleeves, pistons and piston rings, it is the big-end bearings which more often than not are the major components which may give rise to the need for a complete overhaul. This is why access to these parts in the boat used to be regarded as important, and it is a tribute to their long life and reliability that most present-day engines no longer need means of access, with doors in the crankcase; accessibility may be sacrificed for the advantages of lower cost manufacture together with lighter weight and a more compact power unit.

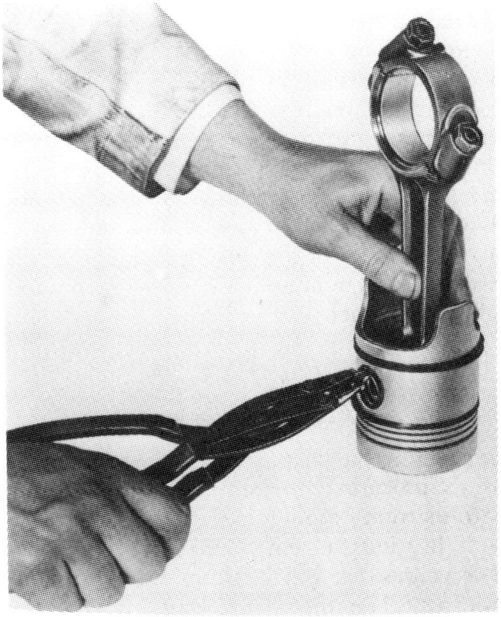

Fig 12. Removing one of the clips which keep the piston pin in place. The pin can then be pushed out by hand if necessary after warming the piston in clean fluid at 100°/120°F (38°/49°C).

Following current automobile practice, the big-end bearings are usually of the pre-finished strip type, comprising two semicircular shells which are clamped together in the lower part of the connecting rod by means of studs and nuts, or by bolts made of high tensile steel. These bolts should always be torqued up to the figures specified by the manufacturers to ensure rigidity of the whole assembly and if specified by the makers, new bolts or studs and nuts should be used each time the big-end is reassembled.

The steel bearing shells in diesels used to contain an antifriction lining material which was a mixture of copper and lead or of lead-bronze. These were bored to the required size when fitted in the rod. This lining material had a much higher load-carrying capacity than the white metal which was once used in cars, but would not tolerate borderline conditions of lubrication. The usual bearings of today's engines are pre-finished to size and are made by a sophisticated process and may comprise layers of steel, copper-lead, indium, tin, etc, some processes of manufacture being patented. This is why the marine engine of today is lighter, cheaper and more reliable than heretofore. The worst things which can happen to big-end bearings and crankshaft main bearings are corrosion, scoring by dirt which has unwittingly been allowed to get into the motor, and inadequate lubrication (due to lack of oil, usually failure to top up).

Connecting rod big-end bearings cannot in any way be repaired, so that whenever they show signs of excessive wear or are scored heavily they must be replaced; makers' figures for acceptable wear are to be found in their manuals. A 0–1 inch ball-ended micrometer is needed to measure wear in shell bearings and can also be used for tubular main bearings, but some skill only acquired by practice is required before accurate measurements can be taken.

Split shell bearings which show signs of wear can be checked by bolting up on the crankshaft with a proprietary product such as Plastigage which, after removal, can then be measured against a chart and instructions supplied with the product. Better still is to measure the thickness of the shell and lining material, but for this you need a ball-ended micrometer.

Tubular bearings such as are used for crankshafts in some engines cannot be measured in this way but there are other methods of checking for wear. The first is the appearance of the bearing surfaces, which normally will show local bright markings if there is wear. If there is severe scoring of the crankshaft and the corresponding bearing, this may be taken as a clear indication to replace the parts. Repair can only be contemplated if there are no more than one or two single scores which are not part of a general deterioration in the surfaces of bearings and crankshaft. The normal wear of crankshaft journals is likely to lead to ovalisation, which can be measured by a mechanic with a fair degree of experience. Trueness must be restored by regrinding the shaft, if replacement under-sized bearings are to be fully satisfactory. A 'bottom overhaul' of the engine is a job not to be undertaken lightly, and when it is done should be done properly with the engine first taken out of the boat. Replacement of connecting rod big-end bearings and regrinding of crankpins would normally be carried out at the same time. Even if it is just possible in some designs to remove these bearings from the engine through an access door in the side of the crankcase, carrying out this type of repair in a small boat is seldom practicable, and the installation of new big-end bearings in this way should only be contemplated in an emergency.

In many engines the lower half cannot be opened up while the unit remains installed. This is particularly the case with some small single-cylinder designs and also with higher powered units based on truck engines. These carry the crankshaft in the combined crank-case-cylinder block casting. It is a measure of the long life and reliability usually achieved with some of these engines that dismantling the bottom-end is not necessary for several thousand hours.

three
Pistons and Rings

There is no component part of an engine more important than any other, since all must function in order that the unit runs and performs its intended task. On the other hand if there are any parts on which this performance is vitally dependent they are surely the piston and ring assemblies. In care and repair, therefore, they must be given proper attention.

Pistons are taken so much for granted since 'every engine has them' and everybody knows what they are or has a notion what they do. A moment's reflection will serve to show how important the piston assembly is. Engine problems such as heavy oil consumption, uneven running, lack of power, poor starting, excessive exhaust smoke or knocking, can all stem from piston condition, so let's take a brief look at their function.

With the connecting rods they form the mechanical link between the fuel burning in the cylinders and its conversion into useful power from the rotation of the crankshaft. We have already described the cycle of operation involving burning of the fuel in the cylinder, which becomes very hot in the process (Fig 6); the piston crowns may reach a temperature of 570°F (300°C) under load.

It should also be borne in mind that the piston has to work under a gas pressure in the cylinder of up to 1000 lb/sq in during the power or firing stroke. Any leakage of combustion gas directly results in loss of pressure and hence of power. To prevent this is the job of the piston rings, or at least those of them known as compression rings, which are at the upper end of the piston. These have quite a tough time of it when the engine is working hard, because the rings have to prevent the hot combustion gases from passing between the piston and the cylinder wall during the (downward) firing stroke. At the same time the lubricating oil from the bottom of the cylinder walls must not pass the other way and be scraped upwards to burn and form soot at the top of the cylinders. For this reason their fit in the piston ring grooves and in the cylinder is vital in sealing both oil and gas; they must also have adequate springiness to exert pressure all round the cylinder walls. Makers' repair manuals usually give recommended figures for the fitting of the rings for the particular engine in question. Typical figures for a 3¼ inch diameter piston are shown in the diagram at Fig 14.

Makers' recommended dimensions should include the wear in the respective grooves in the piston. This clearance is important, more especially for the top ring which, oddly enough, in most motors plays a significant role in controlling oil consumption as well as acting as a compression ring. The scraper or oil control rings proper are usually fitted in the skirt of the piston below the piston pin, sometimes immediately above it. Frequently like the gas or compression rings they are made of high grade cast iron, but sometimes of steel and sometimes of both materials in combination, with a cast iron scraping surface and a steel spring-like expander behind it. The correct size and installation of replacements are important.

Removing the Rings

The task of removing or installing rings is made easier if you have the use of a piston

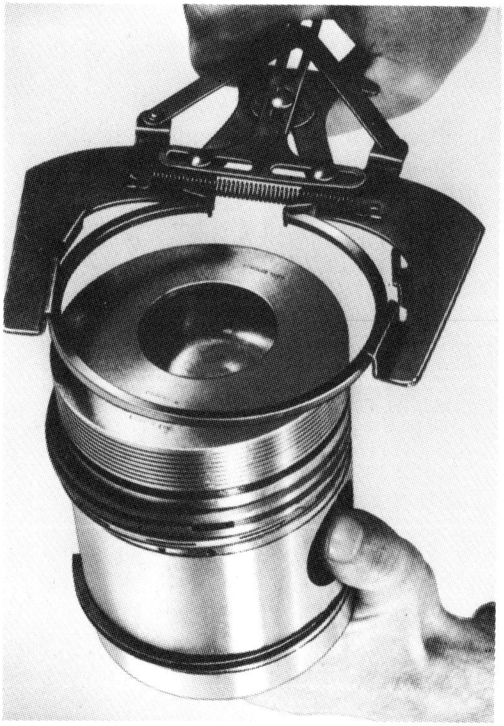

Fig 13. Removing piston rings using expander tool.

ring expander. There are a number of proprietary tools for this purpose on the market which will ease the task without breakage or risk of the sharp ends scoring the piston in the process. So a piston ring expander is a must before attempting to dismantle an engine (Fig 13).

If makers' recommended lubricants and fuels have been used, the amount of carbon or gum deposits in the piston grooves will have been minimised but what is found there, mainly in the upper grooves, must be removed by using a suitable scraper, e.g. made from a file tang ground down to a little less than the width of the groove in question. Care should be used in removing carbon not to score the upper and lower contact surfaces on which the ring seats. If the wear is too great anywhere, the piston must be scrapped unless the makers supply oversize rings. These can work successfully, provided you have access to facilities for getting the pistons correctly re-machined in the grooves so that the 'as new' clearances are restored. The minimum ring gaps should be checked in an unworn portion of the cylinder, near the bottom (Fig 14).

Chrome Plated Rings

It is not unusual for some of the upper compression rings to be chrome plated on those faces having contact with the cylinder walls. Plated rings have been found to have a marked effect in reducing the wear of the

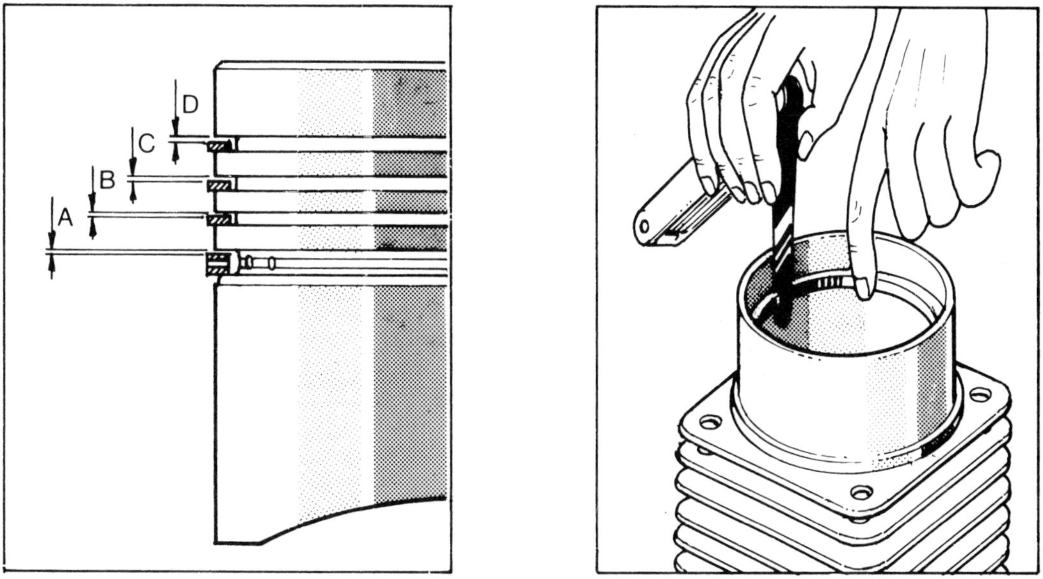

Fig 14. Checking piston ring gaps and side clearance for a 3¼" dia. piston. The recommended side clearances in this case are A) 0.22mm (0.009 in). B) 0.17mm (0.007 in). C) 0.12mm (0.005 in). D) 0.12mm (0.005 in).
The gaps should be not more than 1mm (0.040 in) for the compression rings and not more than 0.8mm (0.32 in) for the oil control or scraper rings. The gaps should be checked with the ring at the bottom, unworn, position of the cylinder.

cylinder liners, but they may require a little longer time to break in from new. They must not be used in conjunction with chrome plated cylinders, because chrome on chrome has been found to be incompatible and seizure will result.

To improve the rate of break in some rings have a taper face (about 1½ degrees) and, if you have one or more of these in your replacement pack, make absolutely sure they are correctly fitted with the etched mark 'TOP' appearing on the upper face, otherwise you will have an efficient oil scraper ring which scrapes the oil the wrong way and so defeats the very purpose for which it is designed.

Oil Control Rings

There is an enormous variety of oil control or scraper rings on the market. To be on the safe side it is as well to use only the engine manufacturer's specification ring packs when repairing engines, since these are known to work satisfactorily. Where these are unavailable, always follow the instructions given with the pack when installing non-proprietary rings.

Piston Materials

The piston has a wide variety of functions. With its rings it has to seal the air space in the cylinder to form the lower half of the combustion chamber, it has to transmit the results of combustion, mechanically via the connecting rod to the crankshaft about 50 times every second. Because of this rapidly repeated cycle it has to be strong, light in weight and at the same time able to withstand heat. Moreover it has to slide in an approximately circular cylinder with ease. These varied functions have been found to be best achieved by the use of an alloy of aluminium. The engine maker has to consider ease of manufacture in addition, so that yet another important factor is introduced into the choice of materials. As a result most makers today use an alloy containing the addition of zinc and tin, or of silicon, which owes its development to the needs of wartime aircraft piston engines and has the required balance of properties. Pistons, some of which are of complex shapes, are produced in a die-casting machine very closely to the finished size, requiring but a minimum of precise machining operations to complete. They are usually finally ground both oval and tapered from top to bottom in order to fit closely in the cylinder without seizure when at working temperature. It is unwise to try to 'adjust' pistons by using hand tools other than to clean them up carefully. For the reason given above they are difficult to measure, apart from the ring grooves, and should be scrapped if they are scored or show signs of severe scuffing or partial seizure on the skirts or in the ring belt. On no account should the ring grooves be wire brushed or sand blasted to clean them.

four
Cylinder Liners or Sleeves

Cylinder liners may be of the wet or dry type, and are usually made of centrifugally cast iron which has fairly good wearing properties. Some engines have been built with liners made of steel which is subsequently chrome plated to give even better wearing qualities. Unfortunately plated liners tend to suffer from problems such as poor oil control and the difficulty of providing an oil retaining surface on the plated finish, and this can lead to scuffing, seizure or high rates of oil consumption, particularly when the engine is new. Chromium plated liners cannot accept some types of piston ring, notably as previously mentioned the chrome faced variety and also steel laminated oil rings with internal expanders. Another reason to use makers' genuine spare parts when repairing or overhauling.

Dry Liners

Dry liners are usually a press fit in the cylinder and those are not easy for the amateur to remove. Fortunately the need for removal and installation of new liners of this type is a comparatively rare event, but it *can* be done by the amateur mechanic. Should the necessity arise, the simplest repair is to have them bored out oversize *in situ* or by replacement of the cylinder block assembly by a 'short' block complete with liners, available from some engine makers or their distributors. Where new liners are installed, their fit in the cylinder block is important, both in the diameter and in the top flange depth, and makers' dimensions must be adhered to rigidly if piston seizures, liner top flange cracking or head gasket problems are to be avoided. (See Fig 15.)

Wet Liners

As their description implies, wet liners have direct contact with the cooling water on their outsides, which helps to promote good all round cooling of the cylinders. The choice between dry and wet liners is largely determined by the general construction of the engine and there are a number of different arguments for and against each type. It is not the purpose of this book to enter into these but rather to point out how these components may best be dealt with in practice; see Figs 7 and 15.

The removal and installation of wet liners is somewhat simpler than replacing dry liners and does not normally require the use of a press, usually a hammer and block of hardwood suffice. However, their fit in the top deck of the cylinder block, and also lower down at the rubber seals which prevent jacket water from entering the sump, are likewise important. Sometimes wet liners show on the outsides evidence of corrosion from the cooling water; a difficult thing to spot without complete dismantling of the engine, and difficult to repair. This corrosion is fortunately quite rare and can be in either of two places. First is pinhole corrosion

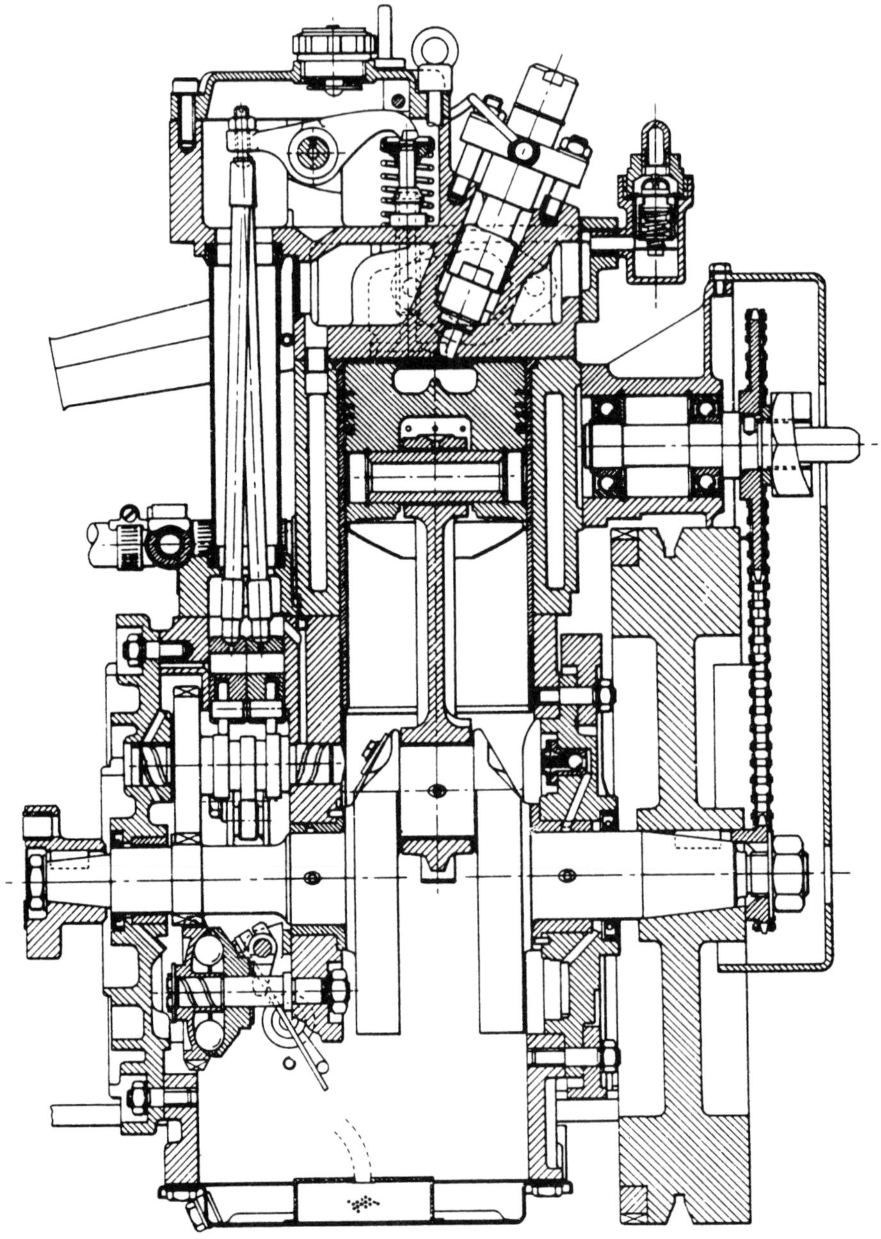

Fig 15. Section of Stuart Sole 9 BHP engine showing replaceable dry cylinder liner construction, also direct injection combustion chamber in the piston.

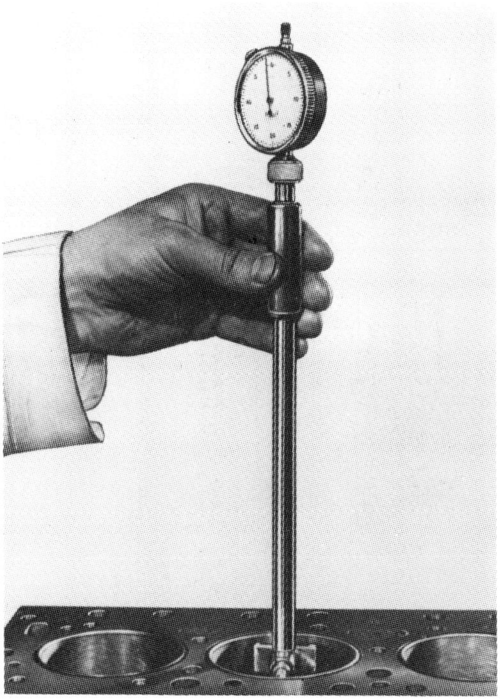

Fig 15a. Measuring cylinders for wear using a Mercer type internal micrometer gauge. Measure the bore at three different places, and check for ovality which should not be more than maker's recommended figure.

which occurs in the barrel, permitting eventual seepage of water into the cylinder. Second is erosion around the lower sealing ring grooves which can permit leakage of water into the crankcase and the lubricating oil. Neither of these seems to be easily preventable by such things as surface treatments by the manufacturers, and they should be looked out for by the diligent repair man since water in the oil or in the cylinder is a certain route to disaster. Persistent loss of coolant follows pressurisation of the water jackets and may be observed in indirect or fresh water cooled engines with a header tank and warrants further investigation. Likewise the appearance of water in the lubricating oil, either on the dipstick or in the valve cover, should be checked immediately. It may be due to a leaky head gasket, or a faulty crankcase breather, or it could be a leak at the liner seals. Should a liner seal be removed for any reason, it must be replaced by a new one and never used again, because they tend to harden and lose elasticity with age.

five
Cylinder Head and Valve Gear

These are important components because they have, like pistons, several functions, the first being to make an explosion-proof lid or cover to each cylinder or cylinders. The second function of the cylinder head is to support the inlet and exhaust valves and their respective operating mechanisms.

Sometimes multi-cylinder engines have separate heads for each cylinder, and others may have castings which cover two, three, four or six cylinders. The relative advantages and disadvantages from the user's point of view of the different arrangements are

Single Heads	*Multi-cylinder Heads*
Smaller individually and less weight to lift off.	In large engines, excessively heavy, necessitating special lifting gear.
More complicated air, water and exhaust manifolding, more joints.	Liable to distortion over length.
Generally simpler to repair.	Harder to make gaskets seal oil, water and gases satisfactorily.
Less distortion, making sealing less difficult.	Some saving in overall weight.

Cylinder Head Maintenance

This is the advice given by one engine manufacturer and, in my view, it applies to all kinds of engine and is thus worth quoting here (the italics are mine): 'The number of hours run has no bearing on when to overhaul the cylinder head of an engine, as carbon beyond a superficial coating does not form and accumulate on the cylinder head and pistons as is the case with a petrol engine. Ease of starting and performance are the determining factors, *therefore the cylinder head should only be removed when it is absolutely necessary.*'

Attention to valves and seats, and in some engines exhaust ports, in the cylinder head is one of the expected forms of maintenance which will nevertheless eventually become necessary after a long period of operation, because there are deposits released on burning the fuel. These deposits contain carbon in the form of soot particles which agglomerate with other combustion by-products to form a solid mass behind the valves. This can eventually lead to sticking valves, poor compression, loss of power and poor starting, smoke in exhaust, etc.

Worn piston rings can result in higher than normal oil consumption, and this in turn will contribute to deposit formation in the areas already mentioned, as the oil is burned. Some oil of course must be allowed to reach the valve stems, the last in the line of the lubrication system, but some makers fit seals to limit the quantity which finds its way down the inlet valve guides. In naturally aspirated engines (i.e. without turbocharger) the inlet tract operates under a slight suction, and excessive oil in this area tends to form deposits on the backs of the valve heads on the stems.

The symptoms of poor compression, poor starting and excess smoke from the exhaust together all point to the need for a top overhaul. Apart from cleaning out the carbon in the area of the valve ports, attention should be paid to the actual seating surfaces of the valves and the seats in the cylinder head. It is important that makers' dimensions and limits be adhered to.

Valves

Valve Seat Inserts. You may find that your engine has inserts fitted in the cylinder head in the position of the valve seats, at least for the exhaust valves which have a tougher working life than the inlet valves and seats. These seats are made of an alloy of iron of better wearing material than the cylinder head itself, but which may be difficult or impossible to recondition by hand lapping (Figs 16a and 16b). At the same time they should wear very little and therefore require less attention than seats machined direct in the plain cylinder head. The general rule of the amateur mechanic must be that if, after cleaning up valves and seats, they appear in fair condition requiring no more than a lick with grinding paste, don't attempt to do any more. If they do not clean up in this way, send the head and valves to a competent specialist workshop. Remember the diesel depends on good valve seating to maintain the high compression needed for maximum efficiency, freedom from smoke and good starting. Should you decide for any reason to fit new valves, it will be important to check their protrusion above and below the face of the cylinder head, because this dimension is closely specified by all makers and if incorrect can lead to untold troubles.

Intake valves are usually slightly bigger than exhaust valves (Fig 17) to improve the engine's ability to breathe the air which it runs on, but it is the exhaust valve which has a tougher life and is more likely to need attention. Skimming the seat face in a lathe usually at 90 degrees included angle can remove most signs of wear (see Fig 18).

If you decide to skim valves, final seating can only be achieved with hand lapping already described. A thin continuous line of contact all round the diameter is better than a wide seat contact area which may take a long time to achieve. Check the fitting of the valve in the cylinder head when work is

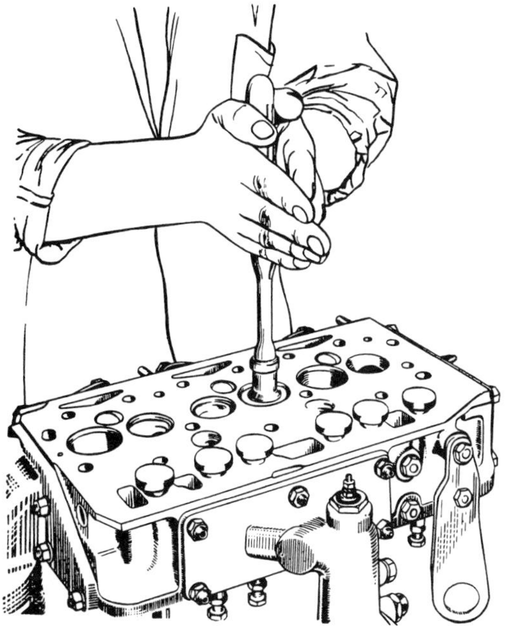

Fig 16a. Hand lapping valves in the seats. Where it is not possible to clean up the seats in this way, resort must be made to re-cutting the seat with a special cutter obtainable from the engine makers or repair shops, as in Fig 16b (Perkins P3M).

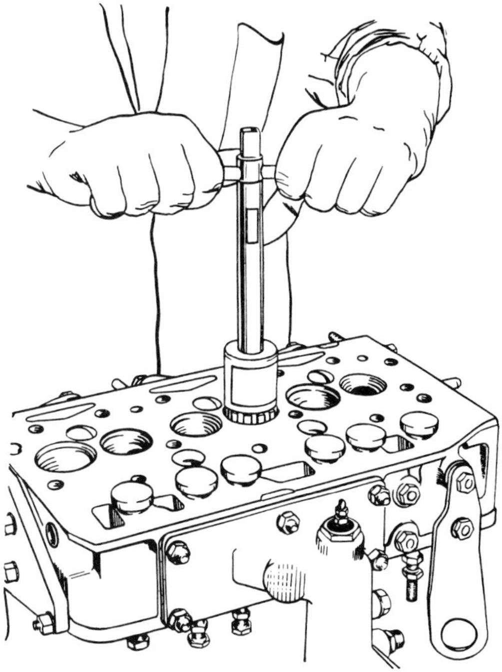

Fig 16b. Re-cutting a valve seat.

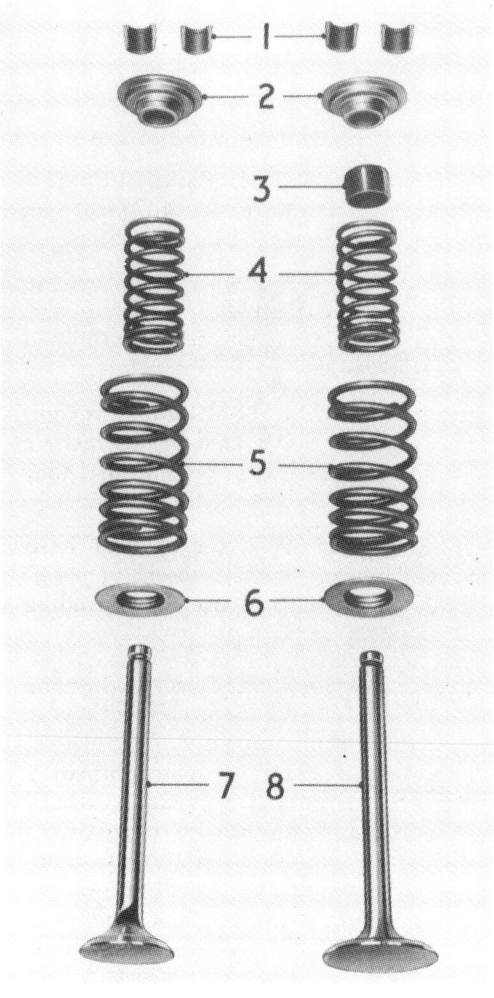

Fig 17. Exploded view of valve components of one cylinder of a Perkins 4.236 engine, showing larger valve of the two (right) for the inlet on which there is an oil seal or deflector 3) which fits over the top of the valve guide.
1) Collets. 2) Valve spring cap. 3) Oil deflector. 4) Inner valve spring. 5) Outer valve spring. 6) Valve spring seat. 7) Exhaust valve. 8) Inlet valve.

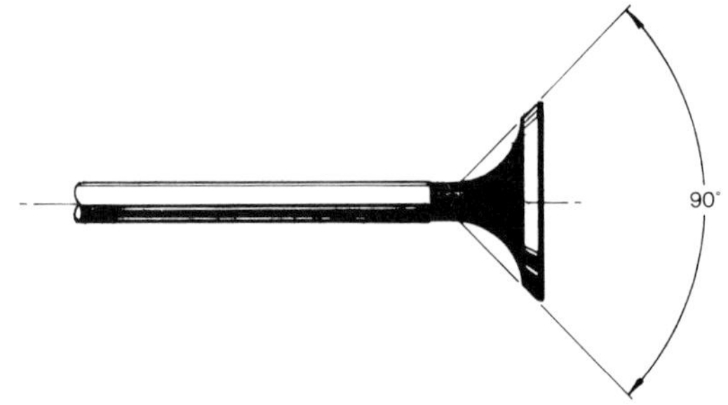

Fig 18. Machining angle for seating face of a valve head.

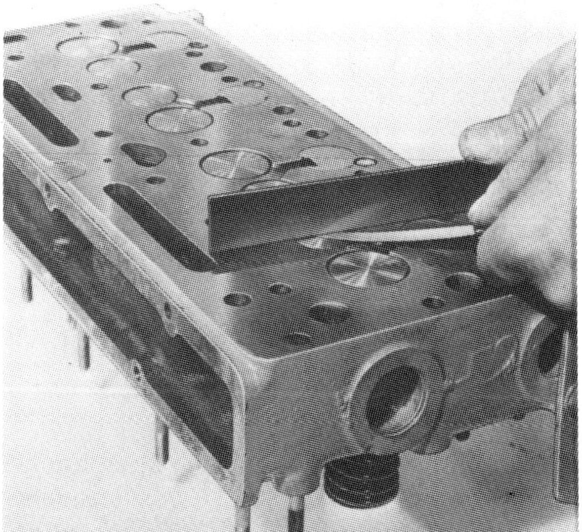

Fig 19. Checking valve depths in cylinder head to ensure that before finally reassembling the head the dimensions are within maker's specification.

completed (see Fig 19). If it has sunk too deeply, some loss of compression will have been suffered and the remedy is to fit a new valve, or a valve and seat insert; in the latter case the job will be probably beyond the average owner.

One further point about valve seats in cylinder heads is that they will have been either frozen when fitting them in position, pressed in or screwed into the head. Whichever method may have been used, you can't get them out without special tools or actually machining them. This is a job best entrusted to the specialist repairer.

New Valves. The old valves will almost certainly have been numbered to facilitate identification. If new valves have been fitted, they should also be marked in the same manner because it is essential they should not be switched once they have been lapped or ground into their own head seat.

Valve Grinding. When grinding in valves which have already been in service, make certain there are no signs of pitting left in the seatings. At the same time care should be taken to avoid unnecessary grinding away of seats in the cylinder head.

1. With valves removed from the head, apply a thin coating of medium or fine grinding paste according to the surface condition of the seat and replace the valve in its guide.

2. Using a suitable suction tool lightly rotate the valve in alternate directions, raising it from its seat from time to time and turning it continuously to ensure a concentric seat (see Fig 16).

3. Add more grinding paste if necessary, and continue the operation until an even matt grey line of contact has been established round a full circle.

4. After grinding operations have been completed, check the valve head depths relative to the cylinder head face to ensure that they are within the maker's specified limits.

5. Thoroughly wash off the cylinder head with suitable solvent, e.g. kerosene or paraffin, and ensure that all traces of grinding paste have been removed.

Valve Guides. Valve guides tend to become slightly bell-mouthed at their ends with wear and are difficult to measure for trueness. Provided there has been adequate lubrication during their life, this is no great drawback and they should not require replacement before major overhaul and not always then. Sometimes there are seals or deflectors on the valve stems to prevent too much oil from getting down the guides where, at the lower ends and on the valves themselves, it will tend to burn and form a gummy deposit. Such seals when fitted should always be replaced by new ones (Fig. 17).

Valve Springs and Rocker Gear. Most diesels have two springs per valve and these take quite a bit of compression to dismantle. With multi-cylinder heads and a number of springs to deal with, you should get hold of a suitable spring depresser, use of which will be much easier than trying to remove the valve collets by using a hammer etc. If you have a single-cylinder engine with only two valves, then you might try removing the collets by a sharp blow with a hide or copper hammer on top of a sparking plug tube spanner placed on top of the valve spring washer or cap; put the head down on a smooth bench for this operation. The cotters should jar out of position on the valve stem and thus free the cap and springs. Care should be taken to collect all the cotters, which have a habit of disappearing.

Valve springs are liable to corrode, especially in a humid atmosphere in the proximity of sea water, so inspect them carefully after they have been washed in solvent before building them back into the engine again. If there is any doubt about corrosion discard them for new ones. If OK, check them for length to make sure they have not acquired permanent 'set' before accepting them for a further period of service. If in doubt – out!

Reassembly

Cylinder Head Gasket. Before refitting the cylinder head inspect the top face of the cylinder block to make sure that the studs, where fitted, are not bent and that the head when offered up slides easily on the studs without interference; also that the block is not cracked around any of the stud or bolt holes in the top face of the cylinder. You may then prepare to fit the cylinder head gasket. There are several types of these available, and it is well to make sure that you have a replacement which is correct for your engine not only by physical examination and comparison with the old gasket, but by checking if the correct part number is marked on it. Gaskets are easily copied and are also the subject of changes or improvements over the years, so make sure you have the correct maker's replacement for your engine.

Whichever type of gasket you have, always fit a new one if the cylinder head has been removed for any reason. Although you may have been careful in removal, head gaskets deteriorate with running and lose essential properties so it is false economy to try to make-do on this item, any leakage from which, whether it be combustion products, oil or coolant, can eventually become an engine stopper.

Jointing Compounds. If the head gasket is a metal one, e.g. copper and asbestos, some jointing compound is probably specified by the engine maker, and it will be advisable to use that one even though there may be others 'just as good', because this is the only way of being sure. Most non-metallic type gaskets (which are becoming increasingly common today) are fitted without jointing compound, so check on maker's instructions again.

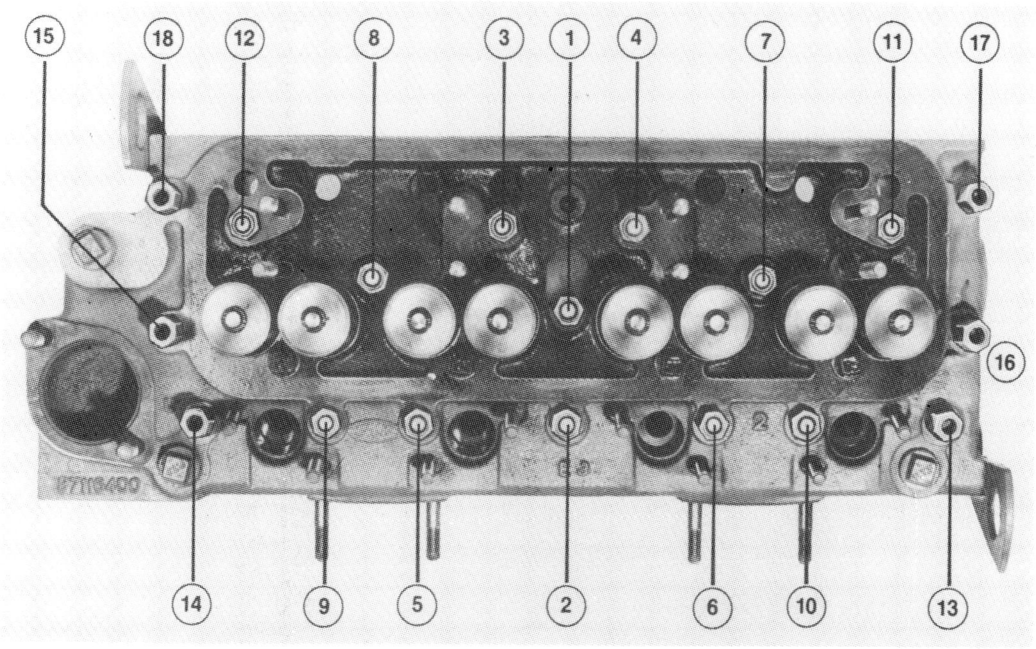

Fig 19a. The final tightening of cylinder head holding down nuts on a 4 or 6 cylinder head is especially important. Here is shown the order, working from the centre outwards, how this should be carried out on a Perkins 4.107 or 4.108 engine.

Tightening the Head. In order to ensure that no gasket leaking occurs after overhaul, the head nuts should be carefully tightened down to the maker's specified torque to give even pressure on the joint face. This is achieved by using for the final tightening of the nuts a suitable torque measuring wrench and working to a set pattern, which in the case of the Perkins 4.107/4.108 engines is shown in the accompanying illustration (Fig 19a). The general principle applies to most engines, the nuts being given a final going over to allow for settlement after the engine has been first run and has warmed up. This applies specially to engines using metal-asbestos type gaskets which tend to squash down rather more than the non-metallic variety.

six
Lubrication System

Correct lubrication of the cylinders and pistons depends on the designer of the engine, who has to see that the right amount of oil is available to prevent metal to metal contact and therefore seizure occurring. What the user can do is to ensure that the right kind of oil is in the sump and that it flows correctly through the filters.

Lubricating Oils

The lubrication requirements of diesels are more exacting than those of other types of internal combustion motor, and that is why oils are specially formulated for diesel engines. It is desirable, therefore, that engine makers' recommendations be followed if best results are to be obtained in terms of trouble-free running and maximum life, because the engine manufacturer will have satisfied himself in conjunction with major oil companies that the lubricants which he recommends meet those requirements. In general, oils sold for the family car will *not do*, but those sold for agricultural tractors and for diesel-powered trucks may be suitable in an emergency.

Additives. Diesel engine oils contain a number of additives among which are anti-oxidants, detergents and dispersants. Anti-oxidants are for the purpose of preventing deterioration of the oil through its being subjected to high temperatures, detergents are for prevention of build-up of combustion products on pistons and in the piston ring grooves and elsewhere, and dispersants are to prevent combustion products from forming accumulations of soot and sludge in the bulk of the oil held in the crankcase and oil sump or pan, and in the valve cover and timing gear case. See Appendix A for specifications.

Viscosity. Viscosity or weight of oil is the characteristic which is a measure of its ability to flow, and it varies a great deal with temperature. Correct viscosity is important at low temperatures to ensure sufficiently fast cranking for easy cold starting, and at high temperature to provide adequate lubrication under full load running conditions. Oils should be chosen having a viscosity which will satisfy as far as possible these two conditions. Engine makers usually specify lighter oils under winter conditions than in summer for this reason.

Viscosity of oils is rated in terms of SAE numbers (Society of Automotive Engineers in the USA). These take both high and low temperature conditions into account. Starting with the lightest (lowest viscosity), SAE 10, SAE 20 or SAE 30 are typical viscosity designations with multigrade designations of, for example SAE 10/30, which combine the best of both worlds. Engine makers specify which grade is the most suitable according to the ambient temperature of operation. The simple principles to remember are that too thick an oil will tend to impair easy starting and to increase friction loss and fuel consumption. Conversely, too thin an oil, while

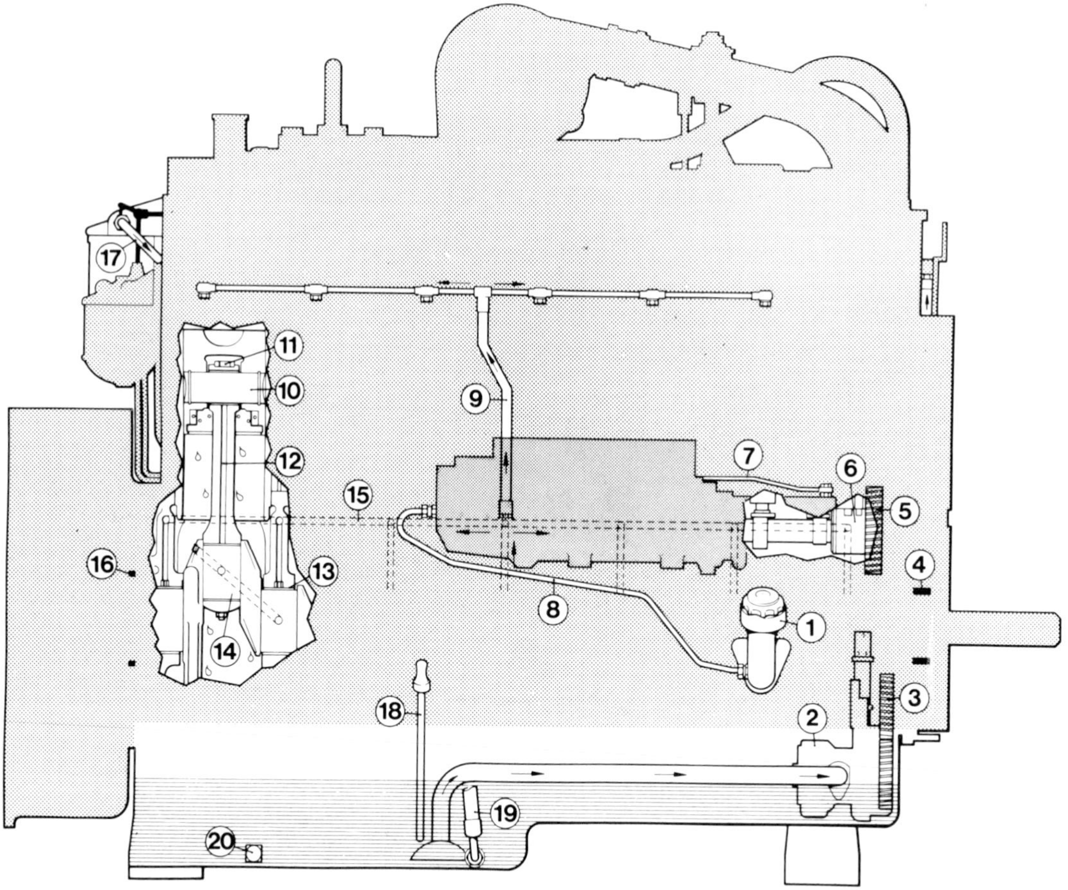

1 Filler Neck
2 Oil Pump
3 Idler Gear
4 Oil Seal (Gear End)
5 Fuel Pump Driving Gear
6 Camshaft Locating Bearing (supplies oil to Fuel Pump Gear)
7 Oil Feed to Minimec Pump (not required for DPA Pump)
8 Return Oil from Minimec Pump (not required for DPA Pump)
9 Oil Feed to Cylinder Head (Valve Gear)
10 Small End and Gudgeon Pin
11 Oil Hole lubricating underside of Piston
12 Connecting Rod
13 Main Bearing
14 Big End
15 Oil Gallery
16 Oil Seal Flywheel End
17 Filter to Turbocharger (HRS/WS engines only)
18 Dipstick
19 Drain from Oil Separator
20 Drain Plug

Fig 20. A lubrication flow diagram for a typical four cylinder engine (Lister HR and HRW).

Lubrication System

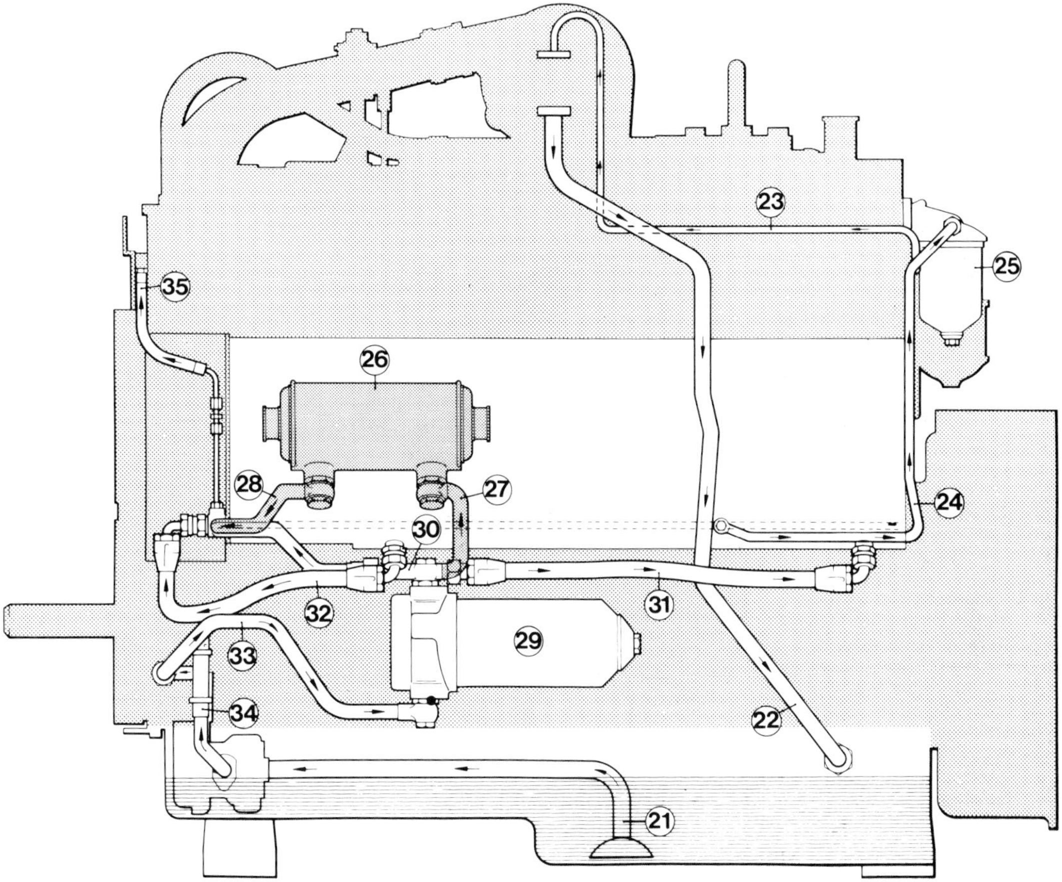

21 Oil Strainer
22 Turbocharger to Sump (HRS/WS engines only)
23 Oil Supply to Turbo-charger (HRS/WS engines only)
24 Oil Pipe-Oil Gallery to Turbocharger Filter (HRS/WS engines only)
25 Turbocharger Filter
26 Oil Cooler (water cooled engines)
27 Oil Supply to Oil Cooler (water cooled engines)
28 Oil Supply to Oil Gallery (water cooled engines)
29 Oil Filter
30 Cooler By-Pass Valve and Pipe (air cooled engines)
31 Oil Supply to Oil Cooler (air cooled engines)
32 Oil Supply to Oil Gallery (air cooled engines)
33 Oil Supply to Filter
34 Oil Pump Outlet Pipe and Relief Valve
35 Oil Pressure Take Off

improving startability, horsepower and fuel economy, will leak more easily, be consumed more easily and may result in a higher rate of wear. That is why it is best to seek engine makers' recommendations and always to carry a spare can on board.

The layout of the lubrication system of an engine is usually quite straightforward and a typical engine arrangement is illustrated in Fig 20.

Oil Levels

In this diagram engine oil is sucked up from the sump by a gear type pump through a coarse mesh strainer, via the suction pipe which is positioned to remain submerged at any angle of tilt the engine is likely to assume while running. That is, provided there is sufficient oil to maintain the level at or above the low mark on the dipstick. It would be unwise to rely on there being any safety margin allowed by individual manufacturers regarding the marks on the stick. Before every trip the level should be checked with the boat on an even keel, as it usually is when on the moorings – not when heeled or when aground. If in doubt, add fresh oil to bring up to the full level, but don't overfill.

Overfilling may cause perfectly good oil seals on shafts to leak which would otherwise remain tight, and other joints to seep oil which once started cannot easily be stopped. The result – an engine which is always a mess and a dirty bilge which is smelly and hard to clean. Another evil which can follow overfilling is an engine which runs hot due to excessive churning in the crankcase with an accompanying loss of power.

I have sympathy with the owner whose engine uses a little oil, not a bad thing in itself, when it is installed below a wheelhouse floor, as is the case with many modern centre cockpit cruisers. The heavy sound-proofed floor has to be lifted up each time the oil level is checked, and that means guests and the rest of the crew being sent and kept out of the way while the operation is performed, sometimes a messy business especially with a twin-engined installation. At least some relief from this routine is obtained if access to the dipsticks is gained through specially positioned holes in the engine covers, large enough to permit the entry of one hand. The main drawback of such a convenience is that sound-proofing measures may be somewhat defeated by a hole or holes in engine covers which are not easily and effectively sealed.

The Oil Circuit

Oil Pump. Having provided the engine with the kind and quantity of oil it needs, let's now look at where it goes and what it does. From Figs 20 and 21 you will see that there is, either in the pump casting or a little further along the circuit, a spring-loaded pressure relief valve. The exact function of this may bear explanation. The engine's actual requirements for oil, which is incompressible,

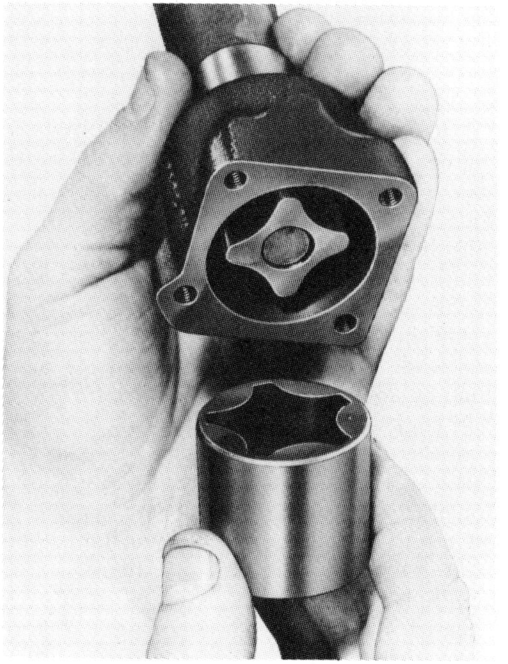

Fig 21a. An oil pump with pressure relief valve in the end cover. Perkins 4.236 engine.

are not always identical with what a pump will deliver; each depends on oil temperature, viscosity and speed of rotation. Therefore the provision of oil by the pump is designed always to be slightly in excess of the engine's needs, with the relief valve letting any excess return to the sump once oil at the pressure required by the engine is available. This prevents any excess output from the pump bursting oil pipes, absorbing too much power and wearing out the pump driving gears.

Oil Pump Repair. Not surprisingly, rotary oil pumps either of the gear type or of the epicycloidal type (illustrated), one or other of which are used in all but the smallest engines, do not often wear out and seldom require replacement, unless there has been an inordinate quantity of abrasive foreign matter passed through them during their lifetime. If this has been the case, by then of course most of the other parts of an engine are worn too. On overhaul, gear and rotary type pumps are sometimes found to have suffered scored end covers and wear on the ends of the gears, which can result in a loss of efficiency (Fig 22). If a new unit is not readily obtainable, this wear can usually be rectified by skimming the end plates. If the pump is worn, setting the relief valve opening pressure higher will not increase the oil supply. The seat of the relief valve, particularly if it is of the ball type, should be examined carefully to ensure that it or the seat is not worn or leaking oil when closed by the spring.

Oil Filters. The oil is first pumped through a full flow filter with a renewable element, which itself has a by-pass which opens whenever it cannot pass oil quickly enough through the element. This occurs either when it is choked with dirt, or temporarily when the oil is cold at start up, particularly in the winter

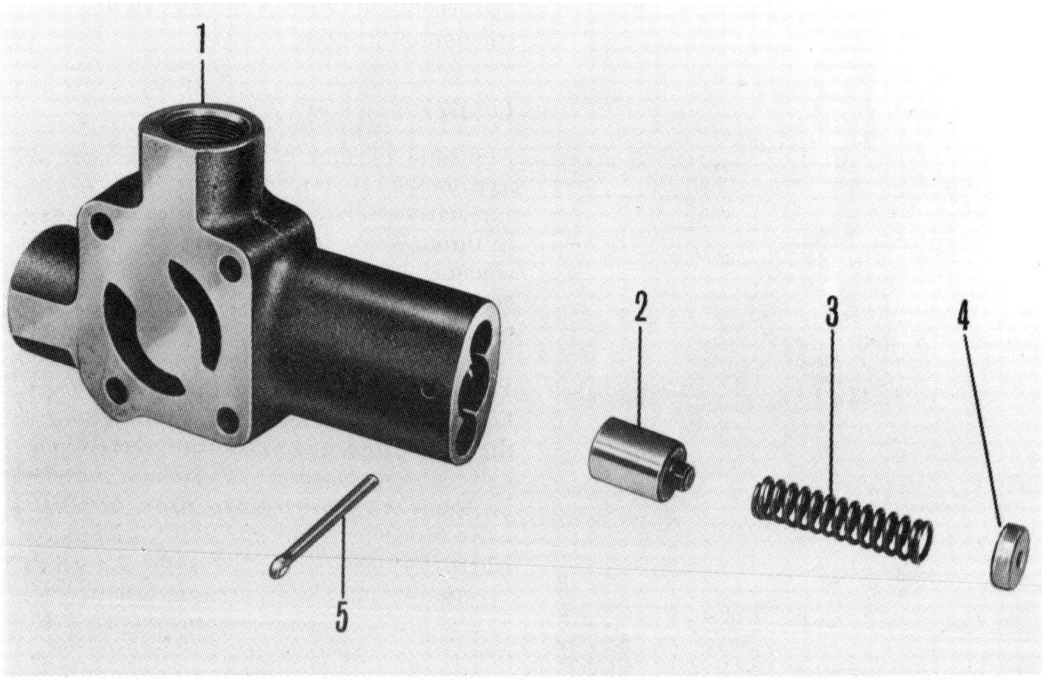

Fig 21b. Exploded view of pressure relief valve assembly.
1) Outlet to main oil filter. 2) Relief valve plunger. 3) Plunger spring. 4) Spring cap. 5) Retaining splitpin.

or if too high a viscosity oil has been used. The remedy for the former is to change the element and for the latter to change the oil itself. Having passed the filter, either through the element or via the by-pass, the oil is ready to perform its work of lubrication and cooling. It is fed direct first to the crankshaft main bearings then to the connecting rod big-end bearings, and thence by splash to the cylinders, pistons and piston rings, where it has its most arduous task to perform. This is the most critical area of the engine requiring lubrication. Temperature and pressure of combustion gases in the upper part of the cylinder and the sliding motion of the piston, which changes in direction about 50 times

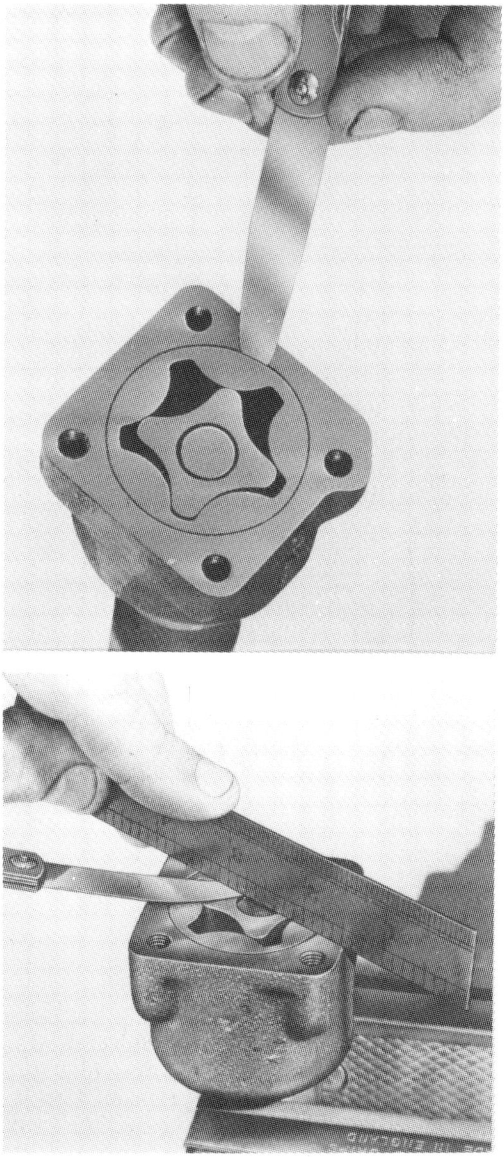

Fig 22. Checking oil pump clearances to ensure maker's recommendations obtain. Clearance between inner and outer rotor should be checked in the same manner as shown top. Perkins 4.236 engine.

per second, all contribute towards the destruction of the oil film.

Lubrication of Auxiliaries

At a suitable point oil is taken from the main feed to the crankshaft and reduced in pressure, either by a restrictor valve or by passing it through one of the camshaft bearings, whence it emerges intermittently to feed the gears in the timing case and the valves and rocker arms.

Valves. Valves are at the end of the oil delivery line, but nonetheless do require lubricating if the guides are not to wear excessively and the valve stems to scuff. Too much oil can cause problems by being drawn down the inlet valve guides and burned on the valve stem, where it forms a sticky carbon deposit which eventually jams the valve from working, and a new train of problems ensues. For this reason most manufacturers fit a valve stem seal, consisting of a rubber thimble-shaped cap which fits on top of the valve guide, and helps to prevent too much of the splash and mist of oil which forms in the valve cover, and on which lubrication of the valve rocker arms, push rods and tappets depends.

Timing Gears. Timing gear drives represent about the only other function of the engine which requires lubrication, usually at reduced pressure, or restricted in flow like the valve gear, and therefore probably from the same supply as the latter. There is usually little to go wrong here and, beyond seeing that the feed holes are clear on overhaul, no maintenance is required.

Oil Filter Maintenance

Now a special word about oil filters. Most manufacturers of diesel engines fit full flow filters in the delivery pipe of oil from the pump to the places where it is used for lubrication; this is in addition to the somewhat coarser kind of filter usually found in the suction line in the sump or crankcase.

The latter you can normally forget. Among other things it is intended to stop a major lump of something left in the engine when it was built, or perhaps dropped in through the oil filler inadvertently when topping up during the course of the life of the engine, and which if it managed to find its way into the oil suction intake would cause lots of damage. Unless you have a problem of excessive sludge formation there is no need for the coarse filter to be cleaned during normal service. If you have a problem of sludge formation you won't get oil sucked up freely and may as a consequence suffer starvation of the bearings. The solution is to obviate the formation of sludge; this was covered in the section on lubricating oils.

The full flow filter is in another category, and regular attention must be paid to this if the maximum possible useful life of the engine is to be obtained. Routine replacement of elements is specified by the makers, because that is the only way to ensure that most of the oil passes most of the time through the filter element. When its resistance is high, that is, when the oil is cold, when the oil is dirty and the filter blocked, the oil passes by the line of least resistance, through the relief valve in the filter head.

Before that moment is reached is the time to service the filter. The makers specify filter change periods and these should be observed. Always keep one spare element on board and then you will not be caught out. Washing of elements in solvents is not usually recommended, because this does not clean them properly and may affect the material of the element. It is far better to fit a new element to maker's specification. After renewing an element, care should be taken to ensure that the rubber rings which seal the metal bowl are in good order and properly installed (Fig 23 a–c).

Spin-on elements are removed by a special tool which is much more convenient to use than trying to adapt conventional spanners, etc. Use care in re-tightening the new element because excessive pressure is not necessary to secure a leak-free seal. Just lubricate the rubber ring before installing and the bowl will turn freely. Check that there is no leakage by running-up the engine after changing the filter.

Draining the Sump. The crankcase oil in the average diesel turns a blackish colour very

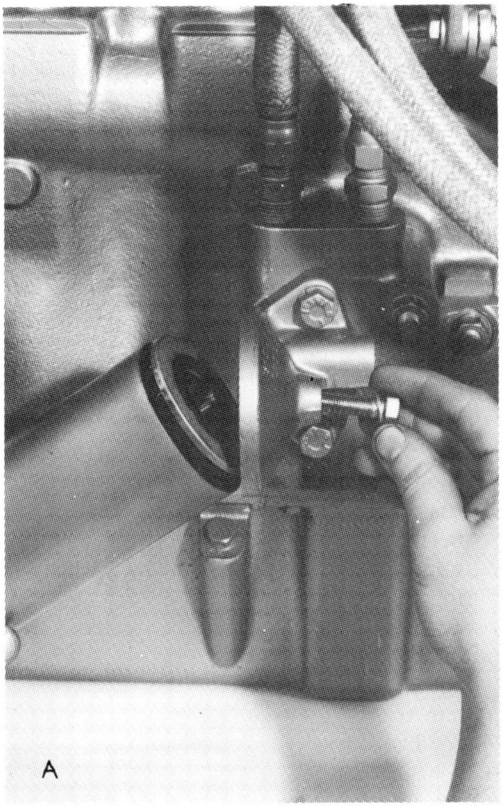

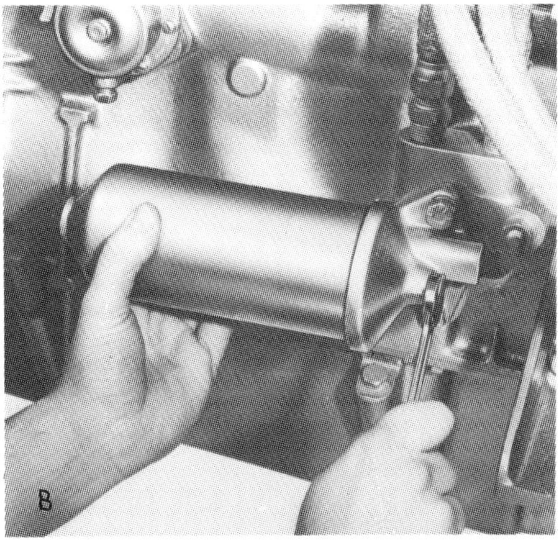

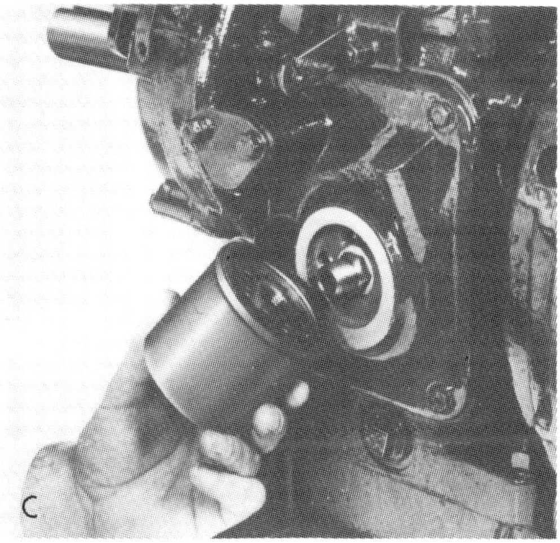

Fig 23a-c. Replacing a full flow oil element. In 23(c) a spin-on type is shown. Difficulty in removal can be quickly overcome if the can is pierced with a screwdriver and it is used as a lever to unscrew it in an anti-clockwise direction, but first make sure you have a spare element (Lister ST1).

quickly due to finely dispersed carbon particles which it holds in suspension. This is quite normal. After a much longer period, along with other waste products and some moisture these may tend to collect in the corners of the engine and eventually may block some internal oil ways. Modern oils keep much more of the unwanted products in suspension and, indeed, some will be filtered out along with dirt and grit by the full flow filter. Usually at the time the filters are due for a change so too is the remaining oil in the sump due for renewal. Much depends on the type of running, so that hard and fast rules for oil change periods cannot be laid down for a given engine, and it is best to follow the maker's recommended practice in this respect. The oil will flow much more easily when the engine is reasonably warm, so give it a run before attempting to suck it out with the pump attached to the engine for the purpose (Fig 24).

If no fixed pump is provided, use a hand pump with a suitably small diameter hard plastic tube connected to the suction end and which can be inserted through the dipstick hole, but remember that it is liable to become too warm to hold with the bare hand if the engine has only just been shut down.

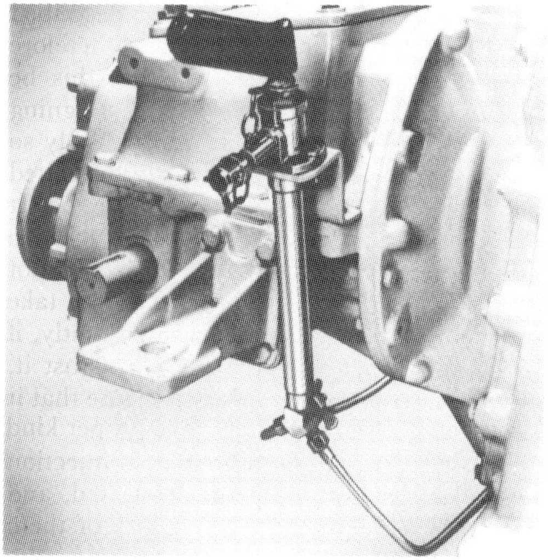

Fig 24. A hand pump permanently attached to the engine for draining oil alternatively from the engine sump or the gearbox.

seven

The Fuel Injection System

The fuel injection system has been described as the heart of a diesel engine and therefore the most important part. Whether this be true or not, the technology behind designing and making it has developed enormously so that it has become a highly sophisticated piece of engineering and very reliable too. It is not surprising therefore that so many take the injection system on trust. This will not do, and I must explain why. You may take the fuel injection pump for granted firstly, if you *don't* tamper with it or try to adjust it, and secondly only if you always ensure that it is provided with clean fuel of the proper kind (see Appendix A). Several makes of injection system and components are illustrated, and much the same rules apply to any of them although their methods of functioning may differ. The level of servicing and attention required varies but broad rules are given.

Filters

The moving parts of injection pumps and fuel injectors are made to an extremely high standard of accuracy, and they depend on very fine clearances between them. For this reason, the fuel itself (which is usually the only lubricant in this area) must be really clean and free from abrasive matter. That is why most systems employ at least one and in some instances up to three filters in the low pressure supply lines to the injection pump, and these must be given regular attention (Fig 25). Filters are usually of two kinds: relatively coarse strainers containing space for settlement of water which can be present in the fuel from bulk supplies, or which gains access to the supply tank, or which is the result of condensation in tanks; additionally there are filters with finer elements made from specially treated paper. Water will tend eventually to block the element of these final filters, which are occasionally duplicated for extra protection. It is best if the settling-out filter for water and larger dirt particles is fitted close to the tank itself, where the water can be checked visually; have a spare glass bowl in case of accident, as it can be dropped by mistake. A jam or pickle jar may do in an emergency, but don't rely on it unless you have first made sure it will fit — a fortuitous and unlikely coincidence I admit; best to have the genuine article. The same goes for main filters — always keep an approved spare element on board (Figs 26 and 27).

Fuel Lift Pump

This low-pressure pump is attached to the engine, and is usually driven either direct or by a push rod from the engine camshaft. Various proprietary pumps are available, and all of them use the same principle (Fig 28). The spring is compressed by the rocker arm or fulcrum actuated by the camshaft; on release it exerts pressure on a flexible diaphragm (of rubberised fabric) which forces the fuel in the pump up into the main filter and thence to the fuel injection pump.

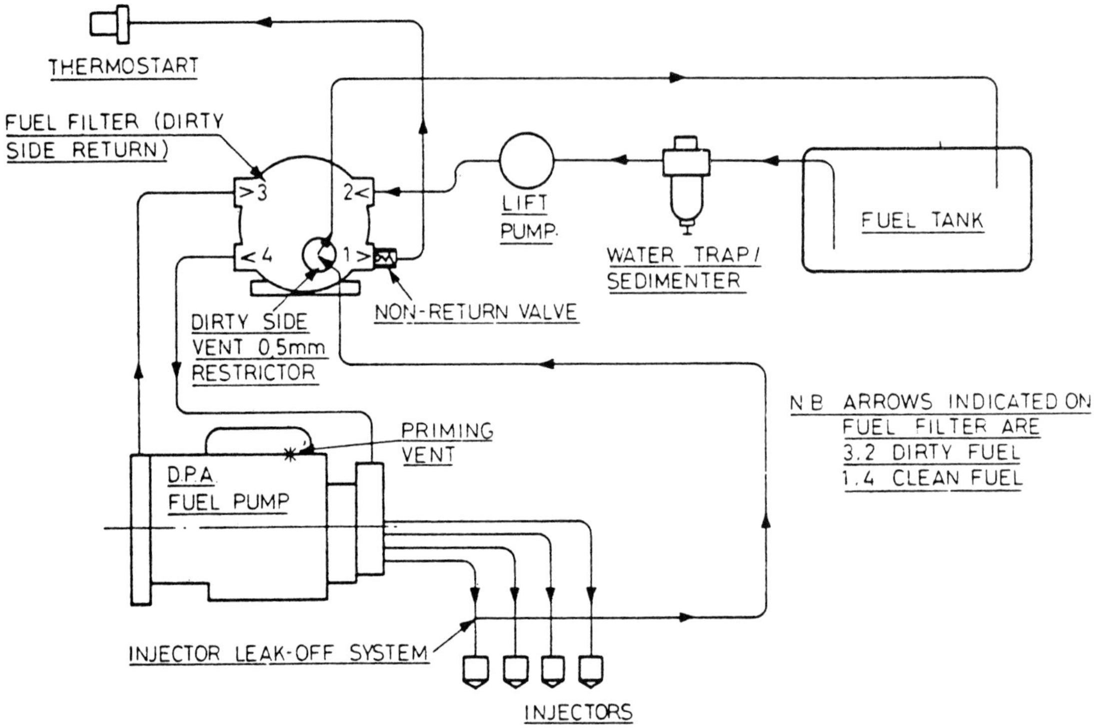

Fig 25. Outline diagram of a typical fuel system for an engine with CAV DPA distributor injection pump.

The lift pump usually has a small, sometimes inaccessible, external lever for hand priming purposes when the engine is stationary. Provided the filters are clean, the lift pump ensures sufficient supply of fuel oil to the main injection pump at a constant pressure predetermined by the strength of the spring. This is sometimes colour-coded so that a replacement spring of the same colour should ensure that the correct feed line pressure is maintained (usually between 5–8 lb/sq in); see Fig 29.

Maintenance. Dirt can accumulate in the feed pump and may affect the action of the two little flat plate non-return valves in the body. The diaphragm has been known to crack and render the pump ineffective, so it is as well to check this occasionally by working the hand priming lever, when the proper action of the pump can usually be felt and heard. If at first there is no effect, turning the engine one complete revolution will be sufficient to ensure that the lift pump spring is not already compressed at the position in which the

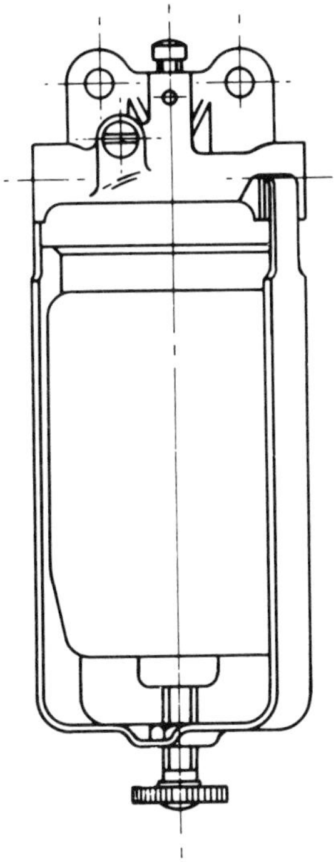

Fig 26. *A water/sediment trap.*

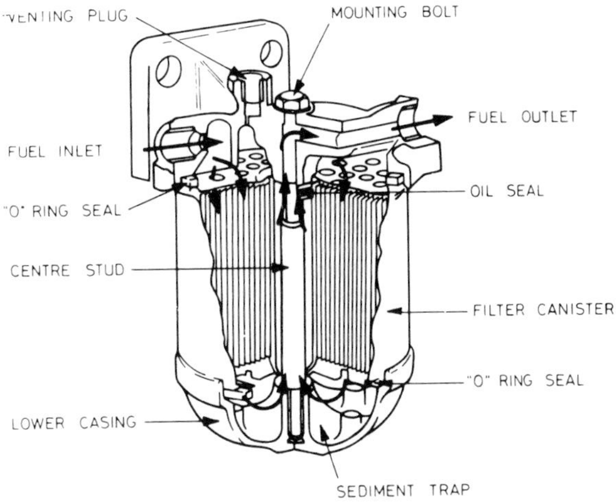

Fig 27. A final filter with replaceable specially treated paper element. The head casting may have a variety of connections, see Fig. 25. Note the vent hole at the top which is the first point for bleeding air from the system.

engine last stopped. Keep a spare diaphragm on board. It is not usually difficult to fit but is virtually impossible to repair or improvise.

In-line Fuel Injection Pumps

In-line fuel pumps are so called because they are made up of single elements mounted in line above a conventional camshaft either within and forming part of the engine or in a separate pump casting for one or more cylinders. Each pumping element contains a steel plunger which reciprocates in a steel barrel, the upper end of which is closed by the delivery valve, as illustrated in Figs 30 and 31. The pump plungers are of the constant stroke variety, and the volume of fuel delivered is varied by twisting the plunger so that the helical slot in its side varies in its position relative to the fuel inlet port in the barrel. The plungers are twisted by a toothed control rod or rack, which engages in each element and moves horizontally under the control of the throttle mechanism or governor

Fig 28. A typical fuel lift pump showing priming lever and extension. (Perkins 4.108).

(Fig 32). Not shown are the roller tappets interposed between each cam and plunger, the tappets being held in contact with their cams by helical springs. Interposed between the outlet of each of the plunger barrels and the injectors is the delivery valve, with its union connection to the thick-walled steel high pressure delivery pipes leading to the injectors.

Maintenance. It is not advisable to adjust an in-line fuel pump when installed on the engine, so it requires checking and servicing by authorised specialist agents. Fortunately the need for attention is normally only after very extended periods of time. This type of pump, originated by Bosch and later made under a number of well-known names, has served the diesel well in the past and is used both in very large and very small sizes of engine.

Distributor Fuel Injection Pumps

For engines of three or more cylinders, increasing use has been made of rotary or distributor type fuel pumps which work on a different principle. The CAV DPA distributor pump which has enjoyed wide acceptance, is illustrated in Figs 33 and 34, and is now standard equipment on many makes of engine made throughout the world.

These pumps are manufactured in two forms, one with a hydraulic governor and one with a mechanical governor; although the basic pump remains the same the external appearance of the two types is different. Both types have been used in marine work, but for most purposes the hydraulically governed type has been satisfactorily used and has fewer moving parts.

The CAV DPA Distributor Pump

Pumping is effected by a single pumping element and, as the name implies, the fuel is

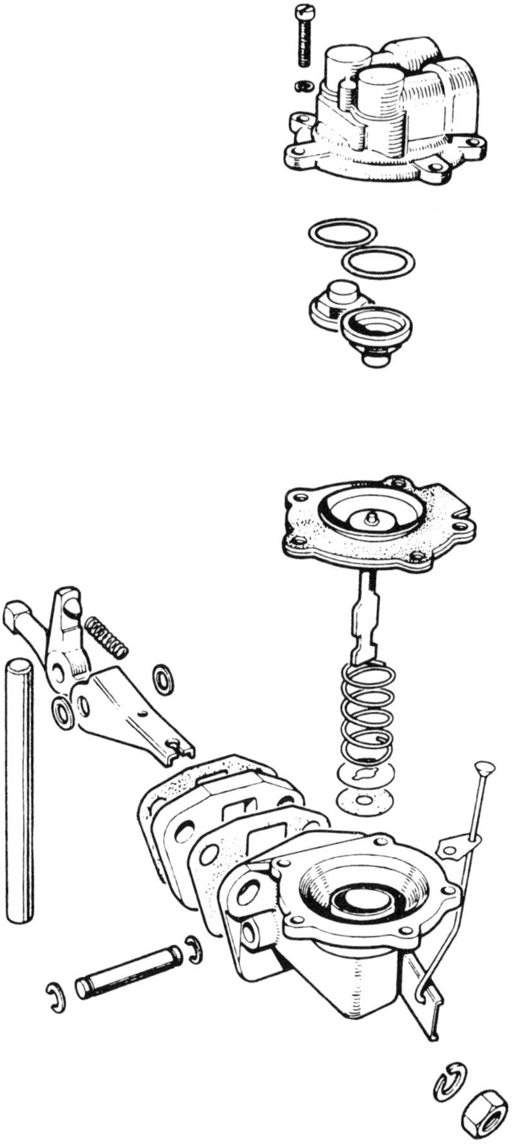

Fig 29. An exploded view of a fuel lift pump (A-C Delco).

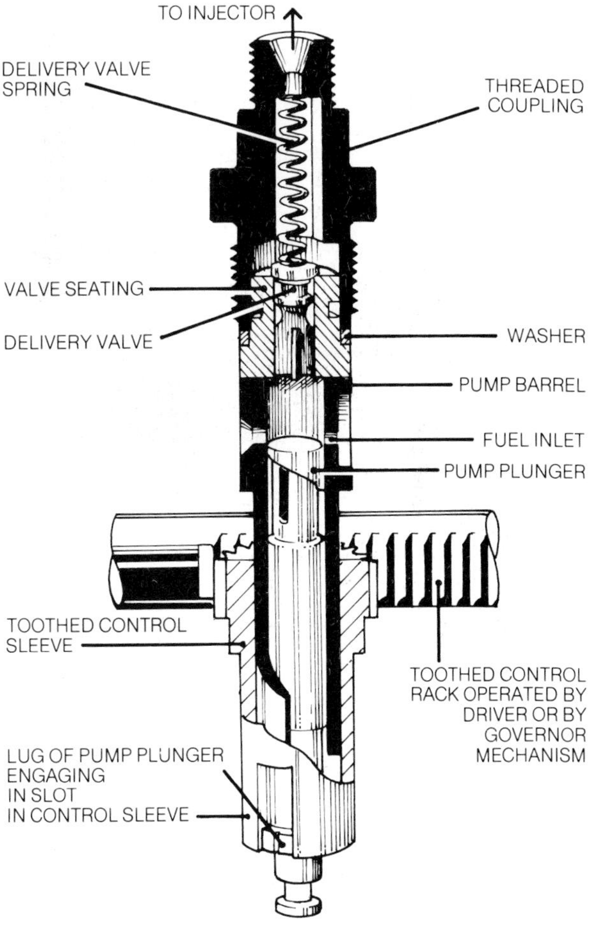

Fig 30. An element containing the pumping plunger of an in-line type fuel injection pump (CAV).

Fig 31. A single element fuel injection pump (Bryce) held in position by a special clamp (Lister).

Fig 32. A multi cylinder pump (Simms) with built in mechanical governor and separate lubrication from engine system fed from pipe A and return via pipe B. Note the anti-vibration clamp on the high pressure pipes.

distributed to each cylinder in turn, being led off the body of the pump by radial drillings and connections evenly spaced round it, at 90-degree intervals in the case of a four-cylinder engine, and 60-degree intervals in the case of a six-cylinder engine. The internal pumping device is simple in principle but there are a number of additional components which all have to do with the built-in hydraulic control system. From the maintenance point of view none of these normally requires attention throughout the life of the engine, because the number of rotating parts are few and those that do move are adequately lubricated by the fuel in which they work. External adjustments can be made to the maximum and idling speeds by means of screws on the upper part of the pump, although on some engines the makers may seal the maximum speed screw in order to avoid the harmful consequences which overspeeding may have on the engine itself. The maximum amount of fuel delivered per stroke is controlled by a sliding adjustment plate which limits the outward movement of the pump plungers. This is situated inside the

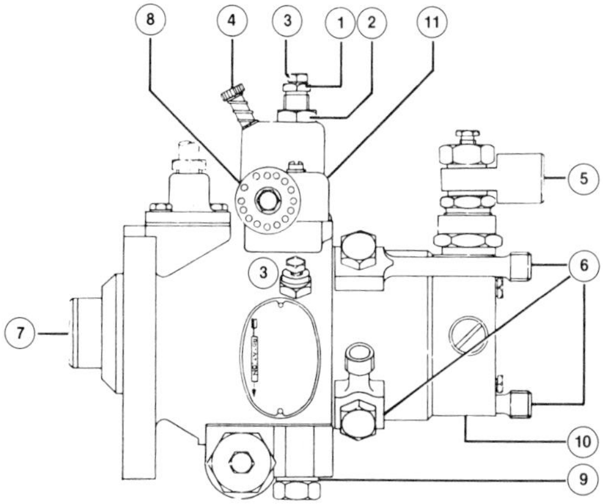

Fig 33. An outline of an hydraulically governed CAV Distributor type fuel injection pump showing main external features. 1) Anti-stall device body. 2) Anti-stall device locknut. 3) Air vent screw. 4) Idling adjustment screw. 5) Inlet from filter. 6) Delivery to atomizers. 7) Drive end. 8) Speed control quadrant. 9) Automatic timing advance control. 10) Transfer pump. 11) Hydraulic governor housing.

pump body and, although accessible through an inspection cover, should never be adjusted in service on the engine and, even after the pump has been removed, only by specialists with facilities for resetting on a pump test bench.

The hydraulic governor is of simple design and is the medium through which the speed of the engine is controlled.

Atomisers

These are sometimes referred to as injectors. The function of the atomiser is to inject the diesel fuel into the combustion chamber in the form of a spray, and an exploded view of a CAV atomiser (Fig 35) with sections through interchangeable nozzles (Fig 36) are illustrated; the various types of nozzle are suited to different types of engine design. Fuel under pressure from the injection pump is fed through the inlet connection down to the nozzle valve seating. The nozzle valve is held on its seating by a spindle and a helical spring, the compression of which can be adjusted so that the valve is lifted off its seat only when the required fuel injection pressure is reached; fuel is then injected through the nozzle into the combustion chamber. Any leakage of fuel at the end of the injection which may accumulate in the chamber surrounding the valve spring is led back to the pump suction chamber, via the leak pipe attached to the upper connection.

The fuel injector nozzle must atomise the fuel properly, and deliver it accurately to the proper place in the combustion chamber. Actual spray shape is such that maximum efficiency will be obtained in the combustion chamber used. In order to fill the combustion chamber properly, direct injection engines (as opposed to the types where the fuel is injected into a separate chamber or annexe to the cylinder head) usually have nozzles delivering two or more sprays radially into the cylinder. Carbonisation and plugging of such

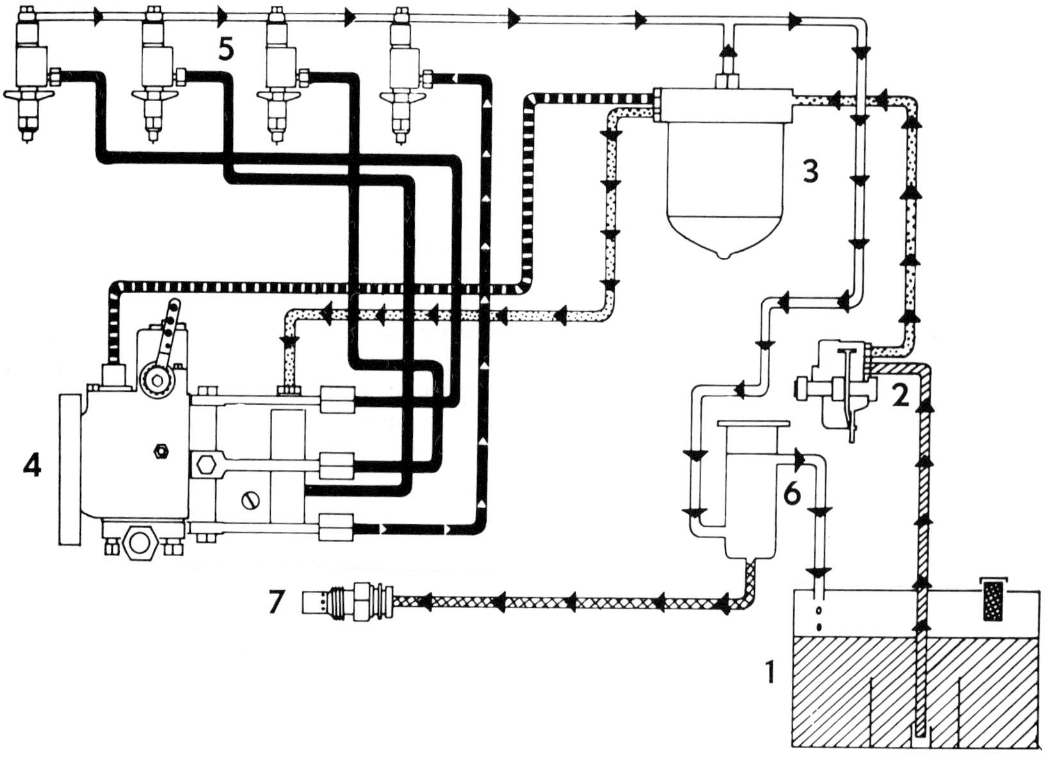

Fig 34. Diagrammatic illustration of fuel system with hydraulically governed DPA pump
1) Fuel tank. 2) Fuel lift pump. 3) Main fuel filter. 4) Fuel injection pump. 5) Atomisers. 6) Starting aid reservoir (when fitted). 7) Starting aid.

nozzles can be a problem and, generally speaking, multi-hole type nozzles require more attention than pintle types which are relatively self cleaning.

The joint between the atomiser and cylinder head is made by a copper washer between the lower face of the nozzle cap and the cylinder head (see Fig 35/12). When preparing to fit the atomiser into place in the cylinder head care should be taken that only

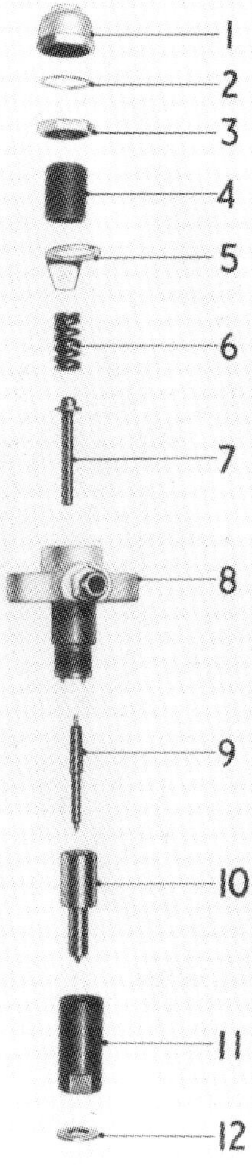

Fig 35. Atomiser. Exploded view of assembly.

the correct copper washer is used to make the joint. The metal of the cylinder head, the faces of the copper joint ring and the corresponding face on the nozzle holder cap nut should be perfectly clean if a leak-proof joint is to be obtained.

It is advisable to fit a new joint washer when the atomiser is replaced after having been removed for any reason. Ensure that the old washer has been removed from the atomiser or cylinder head. The new joint washer should be an easy but not loose fit on the nozzle and, because this is such an important feature, washers especially made for the purpose should be used and no other. On no account should ordinary sparking plug type washers be used.

The atomiser can now be fitted in place, care being taken to see that it is an easy fit in the cylinder head and on the holding-down studs, so that it can be placed down on the copper joint without force of any kind. Even tightening down of the nuts or other fixings should be made with only moderate torques applied. Any tendency to 'blow' when the engine is subsequently started and run at idling speed should be apparent, and the tightening can be finally adjusted if necessary.

Injector Servicing

Maintenance of these parts, so vital to the engine's performance, can be broadly summed up as follows.

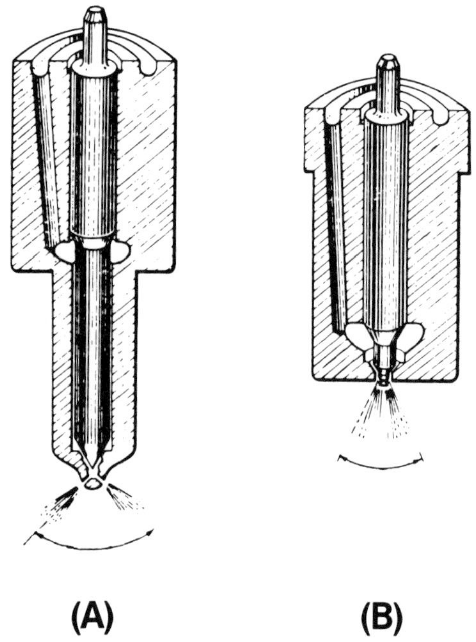

Fig 36. Atomiser nozzles. Two main types: (a) a long stem two-hole type as used in direct injection engines and (b) a short stem pintle type as used in many indirect injection units.

1. Never attempt to take an atomiser to pieces.
2. Have at least one spare atomiser, which has been correctly set for the engine, on board.
3. Learn to diagnose when it may be necessary to change one or more of the existing units.

Here is what one diesel engine maker says, and I quote:

'Atomisers should be taken out for examination at regular intervals. How long this interval should be is difficult to advise, because of the widely different conditions under which engines operate. When combustion conditions in the engine are good and the fuel tank and filtering systems are maintained

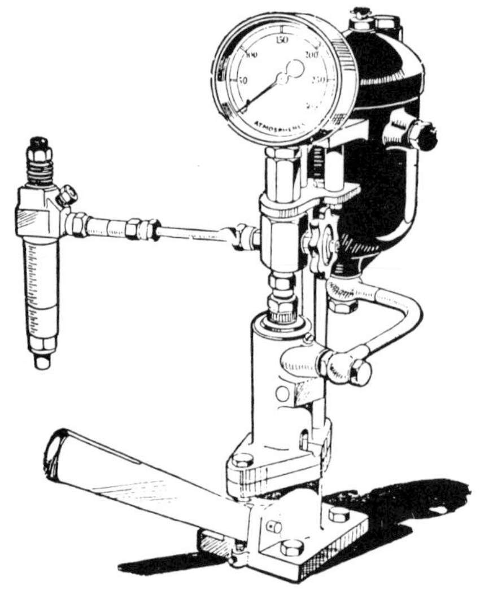

Fig 37. An atomiser testing pump. This is essential for setting up the opening pressures after dismantling, for checking leakage and spray patterns. Great care must be taken in use to ensure that no part of the spray penetrates the skin of the hands. In this event immediate medical attention is called for.

in first-class order, it is often sufficient if the atomisers are tested every 1,000 hours.'

It is no use taking atomisers out for attention unless the proper servicing equipment is available, or spare atomisers are at hand for substitution (Fig 37).

The nearer the ideal engine conditions (good fitting with adequate cooling and absolutely clean fuel) are realised, the less attention the atomisers will need, and so the longer will be their efficient life. In this connection, since there is no other item of equipment on which the performance of an engine depends so much, it pays the user handsomely to see that the engine never runs with any of its atomisers out of order.

Injector Fault Finding. The first symptoms of atomiser troubles usually fall under one or more of the following headings:

1. Misfiring
2. Knocking in one (or more) cylinders
3. Engine overheating
4. Loss of power
5. Smoky exhaust (black)
6. Increased fuel consumption

Often the particular atomiser or atomisers causing trouble may be determined by releasing the pipe union nut on each atomiser in turn, with the engine running at a fast tick-over. This should prevent fuel being pumped through the nozzle to the engine cylinder, thereby altering the engine revolutions. If after slackening a pipe union nut the engine revolutions remain constant, this denotes a faulty atomiser.

After stopping the engine, the nuts from the flange of the doubtful atomiser should be removed and the complete unit withdrawn from the cylinder head and turned round, atomiser nozzle outwards, and the unions retightened. After slackening the unions of the other atomiser pipes (to avoid the possibility of the engine starting), the engine should be turned until the nozzle sprays into the air, when it will be seen at once if the spray is in order. If the spray is unduly 'wet' or 'streaky' or obviously to one side, or the atomiser nozzle dribbles, remove from the fuel pipe; the faulty atomiser should then be securely wrapped in a plastic bag for attention on the maintenance bench.

Great care should be taken to prevent the hands or face from coming into contact with the spray, as the working pressure will cause the fuel oil to penetrate the skin with ease.

High Pressure Fuel Pipes. After replacement of atomisers in the cylinder head and reconnection of pipes at the unions, any tendency for these to leak should be checked as the next operation. The nuts should not be overtightened and, provided the pipes themselves have not been bent or disturbed when the atomisers were removed, they should seal satisfactorily. Proper injection will not take place if they do not seal effectively and the olive connection at the end should be examined to see that there is a satisfactory contact mark

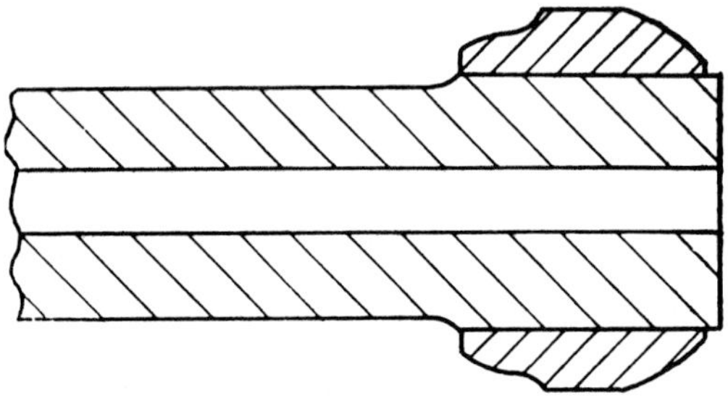

Fig 38. An enlarged view of a high pressure fuel pipe end. The steel pipe is fitted with a brass olive which is specially shaped and deforms when clamped by the union nut to form a leak-free joint. Avoid excessive tightening.

round its periphery and it is not loose on the pipe. If in doubt renew the olive. Keep a few spare olives on board (Fig 38).

It is a good practice to keep a spare set of pipes on board or at least one pipe pre-cut to the correct length and made up with end fittings, which can be bent to suit in the rare event of a crack or fracture occurring. Such failures when they do happen are almost certain to have been the result of metal fatigue due to vibration and, where there is known to be a vibration problem the pipes will have been joined together at a suitable point with clips or clamps or secured to the engine structure by a bracket. The screws of any clamps should be checked periodically for tightness — the best insurance against this type of failure. Finally don't try to hammer up the end of a fractured pipe to stop it leaking. Even if you are successful in stopping the leak, you will almost certainly cause an hydraulic lock in the fuel pump with possible serious consequences.

Leak-off Pipes. The leak-off pipes should be connected up finally after the main high pressure connections have been made. New washers should be used on the banjo bolts where fitted, and then the engine run again to check for leaks.

Bleeding the Fuel System

In the event of air entering the fuel system, it will be necessary to bleed the whole system before starting can be effected. Air locks can be either due to running out of fuel or leakage on the suction side of the supply line. If you have an engine which is an auxiliary, the suction pipe in the tank can be uncovered when you heel, even if it is immersed when on an even keel.

To bleed the system, unscrew by two or three turns the vent plug on top of the fuel filter cover (not the return pipe to the tank) (Fig 39).

Slacken the vent screw on the hydraulic head locking screw on the side of the fuel injection pump body (Fig 41).

Slacken the air vent screw near the top of the governor housing on the fuel injection pump. Ensure that any anti-stall device which may be fitted is not disturbed (Fig 42).

Operate the priming lever of the fuel lift

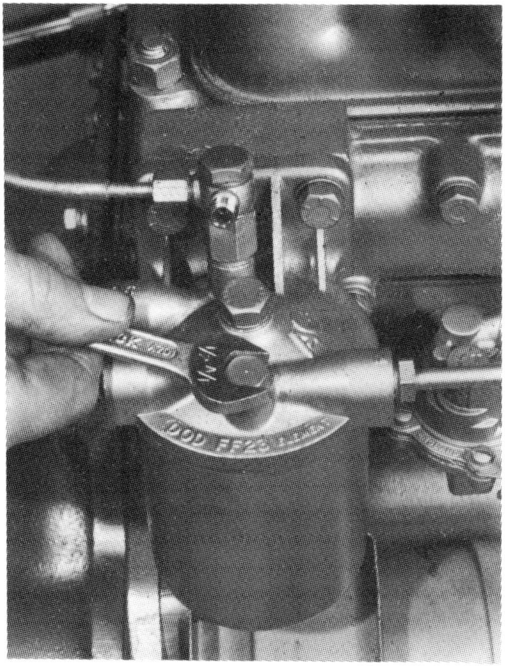

Fig 39. The air bleed screws on the fuel filters. Practice should be gained in carrying out this operation which may become a necessity at any time the engine stops or fails to start.

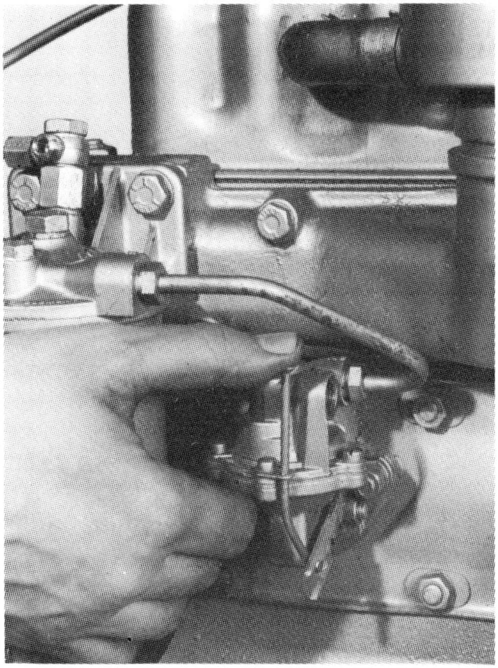

Fig 40. Operating the priming lever on the lift pump.

pump (Fig 40). If the cam on the engine camshaft driving the fuel lift pump is on maximum lift, it will not be possible to operate the hand primer, and the engine should be turned one complete revolution. When fuel, free from air bubbles, issues from each vent point, tighten the connections in the following order:

1. Filter head venting screw (if fitted).
2. Head locking screw on fuel injection pump.
3. Governor vent screw on fuel injection pump.

Slacken the pipe union nut at the fuel injection pump inlet, operate the priming lever on the lift pump. Re-tighten when fuel,

Fig 41. Bleeding air shown being carried out with a CAV distributor pump (also Fig 42) with hydraulic governor; this will be necessary with all types of fuel injection equipment – see maker's instruction book. Here the bleed screw gets a turn.

Fig 42. The bleed screw on the governor housing.

free from air bubbles, issues from around its threads (Fig 33/6).

Slacken the unions at the atomiser ends of the high pressure fuel pipes.

Set the throttle in the fully open position and ensure that the stop control is in the 'run' position.

Turn the engine with the starter motor until fuel oil, free from air bubbles, issues from all fuel pipes. Some 30 to 60 seconds of rotation may be necessary before this condition is reached, and the time will be dependent on speed of rotation and effectiveness of the bleeding operation described previously. A fully charged battery in a temperate or warm climate will rotate the engine at upwards of 280 rpm and, under these conditions, the remaining air should be expelled in under 30 seconds. Cold conditions or partially discharged batteries may take longer.

Tighten the unions on the fuel pipes, and the engine is ready for starting.

If after bleeding the engine starts and runs satisfactorily, but after a few minutes it stops, then it can be assumed that air is trapped in the fuel injection pump. The bleeding procedure should be repeated, at the same time checking for air leaks on the suction side, such as loose connections or faulty joints.

Priming Procedure after Changing a Filter Element

Note: Where the fuel filter cover does not incorporate a vent screw, the priming of the fuel filter is automatic.

1. With the vent screw (if fitted) on the filter cover removed, and the union at the filter end of the return pipe (filter to tank) slackened, operate the feed pump priming lever until fuel, free from air bubbles, issues from the filter cover vent.
2. Replace the vent plug, and continue to operate priming lever until fuel, free from air bubbles, issues from around threads of return pipe union.
3. Tighten the return pipe union.
4. Slacken the union at the filter end of the filter to the injection pump feed pipe, and operate the priming lever until fuel, free from air bubbles, issues from around the union threads.
5. Tighten the feed pipe union. Pump and filter are now filled and primed.

Fuel Oil

The importance of clean fuel passing through your fuel injection pump and atomisers cannot be too strongly emphasised. All fuel used in the engine must be uncontaminated and should conform to the specification given by the makers of the engine.

Some applications have a gauze trap in the filler of the fuel tank. This must not be removed when fuel is being poured into the tank. If there is no filter in the filler opening and any doubt exists as to the cleanliness of the fuel, the fuel should be poured through a fine gauze strainer.

Do not store fuel oil in a galvanised container.

Other Types of Fuel Injection Equipment

Some current designs of small marine diesels employ fuel injection equipment which has been developed primarily to meet the needs of the small car/light van market. Among these are the Bosch EPVE and the Lucas-CAV DPS rotary fuel injection pumps. These fuel pumps are highly sophisticated in design and offer the facility of running up to 6000 rpm, something not required of marine engines. However, they have other additional features which are required in the marine environment. These are, for example:

1. Automatic excess fuel and adjustment for timing in cold starting situations and a cold idle advance device controlled by a waxstat.
2. Built in 'ignition key' operation for starting and stopping the engine.

3. Automatic air venting to cope with running out of fuel or leaks in the low pressure fuel line.
4. A boost control device for turbocharged engines. This reduces fuel delivery at low boost pressures and hence reduces exhaust smoke.
5. A torque control device for altering the fuel delivery curve shape over the speed range where additional BHP at maximum speed is required.

None of these features affects the simple principles of care of the fuel system already described in detail, but in terms of maintenance, because of the increased complication, the user is all the more forced into the hands of the specialist agent appointed by the maker of the equipment.

eight
Intake Systems

Air is free for the taking, but it must be remembered that it is an essential commodity for combustion, and the only stipulations are that there should be no restrictions in getting it to the engine and that it must be free from dust and dirt and reasonably dry. These requirements are often taken for granted in a marine engine, and it is probably true that they are met for the majority of engines operated on the seaboard. The makers of so many of the marine engines on the market today have, however, tended to ignore the air cleaning side of the engine. Anyone who has experience of operating engines in desert conditions knows just how quickly machinery can become 'clapped out' after a few sand storms.

The reader might well ask 'What has that to do with marine engines which operate on the water?' To which I would reply 'What about those marine engines which operate on the Nile, which in places passes through desert, and in many other parts of the world where land dust is carried out to sea in enormous quantities due to the prevailing winds? What about the river Thames passing through the heart of London? Or the sea off Los Angeles with its smoggy atmosphere? Is there not some risk of dust being carried into the boat engine's intake?' It is a question of degree how much your engine is exposed to the risk of prematurely wearing out and, if it is not fitted with an air cleaner, you might well judge one to be a worthwhile additional piece of equipment (Fig 43).

Air Filters

Damage to the wearing surfaces of an engine can quickly take place if any quantity of dust enters the intake, notably scoring of pistons and cylinders, wear of piston rings, and sometimes wear of soft metal bearings, in any case shortening the overhaul life of the engine. Damage can even come from the air intake filter itself if it is of the metal gauze type: salt air corrosion can cause particles to break loose as it eventually disintegrates, to be carried in the air stream into the cylinders.

Outside intake systems ducted direct into the engine must be capable of separating water from air, or otherwise must be adequately baffled to make sure no water can enter the engine, but be assured humid sea air can be difficult to avoid, so regularly inspect the whole intake systems of boats which operate in salt water.

Intake Silencers. Some engines are fitted with intake silencers which may or may not combine with air filters. The interior of these, which often silence because of their shapes and volumes, should be examined for rust which if dislodged can be unkind to engine pistons and cylinders. Sometimes gauzes are fitted to prevent large foreign objects from gaining access to the intake manifold. The gauzes can do more than a little harm if they are not proof against rusting, so take a once a season look at these to make sure they are not rusting and breaking up due to vibration.

To sum up, therefore, engines installed in

Fig 43. A dry air cleaner showing renewable paper type element (Lister).

separate engine rooms, or under floors of wheel houses, are unlikely to suffer too much from the effects of high dust concentrations (with the exception of those normally operating in territories such as parts of the Middle East) and do not require special protective measures. Where these are needed, the intake filters or air cleaners should be constructed of materials which are not liable to suffer from corrosion. Paper elements should be of material which has been protected from absorbing moisture. Operating conditions will largely determine service intervals. Note should be taken of the engine maker's recommended periods for cleaning existing air filters as stated in their instruction literature. The important thing is not to forget all about the intake system. Keep it on your list of regular inspections.

Turbochargers

Turbochargers are widely used today to increase the power of naturally aspirated engines. There has been a certain amount of caution, not to say prejudice, against the use of turbocharging when applied to smaller high speed diesels (of 60–120 hp) to augment their power. This increase can be achieved in most cases without running the risk of any reduction in engine life and reliability, provided the engine makers supply the engine fitted with a turbocharger in the first place. The fitting by amateurs of turbochargers to existing engines is not recommended because, among other things, additional cooling capacity may be required (Fig 44).

A turbocharger consists of a vaned impeller or rotor which runs in a scroll shaped casing forming an air compressor. On the same shaft as the compressor rotor is another rotor made in heat resisting steel, which rotates in another casing forming the turbine half, driven by the exhaust gases from the engine. The unit is usually mounted on, or is attached to, the exhaust manifold. The shaft and rotor assembly are within close limits of

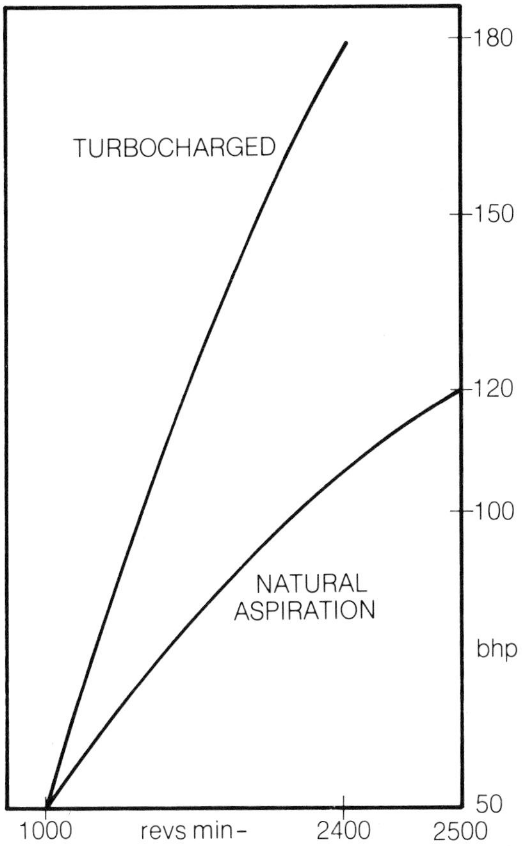

Fig 44. Graph showing the effect of turbocharging a 120 b.h.p. 6 cylinder engine, increasing power to 180 b.h.p. Note the relatively insignificant power increase at low speeds.

balance and therefore wear of the bearings should be minimal, but these should be replaced as soon as there is any sign of rubbing of impellers on the casings.

The turbocharger is basically a simple component (Fig 45) but it may run up to 100,000 rpm and relies upon proper design, special materials, precision manufacture and finally correct matching to the engine to provide the degree of power increase which goes with the increased air supply to the cylinders. This increase of power can only be achieved by also matching the supply of fuel. An engine intended to give, say, 30 per cent more power when turbocharged will need approximately 30 per cent more fuel at full throttle, so that injector and fuel pump setting will be modified accordingly. Notable also will be the need for increased availability of water for cooling, and this means not only the cooling of the cylinder jackets but also cooling of the turbocharged intake air. Unfortunately, by one of those laws of nature which seem to prevent us from gaining something for nothing, the air which leaves the turbocharger is not only under pressure but has become hotter as it has been compressed, and so it must be cooled if it is to be of maximum benefit to the engine (Fig 46).

This cooling of intake air is achieved by passing the air from the turbocharger through something rather similar to the oil cooler. It consists of an outer casing through which a bunch of small water tubes of about ¼in diameter pass. The coolant is sea water,

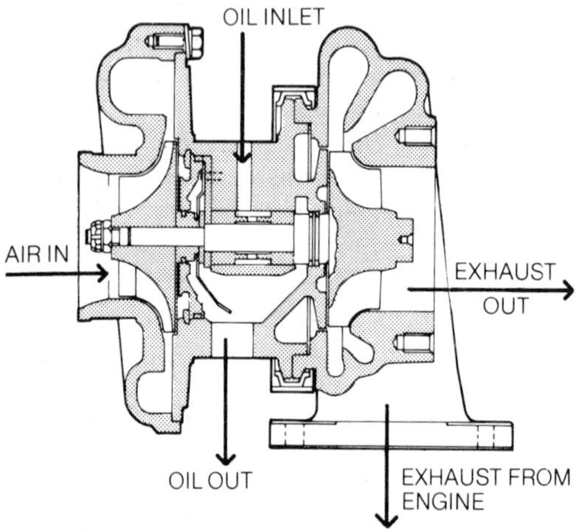

Fig 45. Sectional drawing of a turbocharger. The air outlet from the compressor scroll is not visible in this view (Holset).

so that it is always plentifully available and relatively cool.

Maintenance. Care is confined to ensuring that clean oil reaches the bearings in the required amount. The oil feed is sometimes taken from the clean side of the main engine filter, sometimes it has its own special filter. In either case the filter should not be allowed to become blocked before replacing the element, so that adequate oil supply is available at all times. If the system is dismantled for any reason, the oil supply to the bearing should be suitably primed before starting up to ensure that bearing seizure does not occur. The oil must be allowed to get away after doing its job, and therefore the drain pipe must not be blocked or restricted, or the seals at the ends of the shaft will be overloaded and leak oil where it is not wanted.

Here are the service checks advised by one manufacturer of turbochargers and which will serve as a guide:

Loss of power, excess smoke, high fuel consumption, overheating, high exhaust temperature, oil leakage from the turbocharger, are all symptoms which could indicate turbocharger malfunction. These faults, however, are often wrongly attributed to the turbocharger, because defects in other components can produce the same symptoms. Since the turbocharger cannot be adjusted or regulated, only mechanical damage or blockage due to dirt can impair its performance. Before replacing a turbocharger, therefore, the following points should be checked:

1. *Air Filters.* These must be properly maintained. A blocked air filter will restrict the air flow to the compressor. An inadequately maintained air filter will cause fouling of the compressor.

2. *Joints and connections.* Check for gas leakage at the exhaust manifold or turbine inlet. Check for air leakage at the turbocharger air outlet connection and engine air manifold joints.

3. *Oil leakage.* The prime cause of oil leakage

Fig 46. View of a Mermaid marine diesel of 130 b.h.p. at 2500 revs. min. fitted with Borg Warner reverse and reduction gears. This shows clearly the Holset 3LD turbocharger with heat shield over the turbine and pressure feed for oil entering the bearings from the top. Also shown are 1) the gearbox oil cooler, 2) the engine oil cooler, 3) the charge air cooler, and 4) the combined header tank and water heat exchanger for engine jacket cooling.

from the turbocharger is a blocked air filter. Also check for damaged or badly fitted oil pipe connections. Since oil is drained from the turbocharger under gravity, a blocked or damaged oil drain pipe may cause a build-up of oil in the bearing housing. High crankcase pressures in a worn or damaged engine will also restrict the flow of oil from the bearing housing.

4. *Fuel injection equipment.* Faulty operation of the fuel injection equipment will result in loss of power and excessive exhaust smoke. The injectors should be examined and cleaned if necessary, and the pump calibration checked.

The benefit of a turbocharger is best felt at wide throttle openings when maximum power is required. Under this condition the boost pressure gauge usually fitted with such engines will read its maximum. This may be of the order of 3–4 lb sq in. At lower speeds don't be worried if the boost pressure is less, or even zero; there is no point in having an excess of boost at part throttle. Zero boost at full throttle means that the rotor is jammed or more likely there is a major leak in the intake system, e.g. a joint on the flange connecting the intake manifold to the cylinder head, or a flexible hose or hose clip on the air delivery side of the turbocharger. The characteristic whine of the turbocharger may rise in note if this occurs and is indicative of overspeeding; loss of boost pressure at full throttle will be accompanied by loss of power and excessive smoke from the exhaust. In this case the engine should be shut down and the cause establised.

Repair. Like much of the electrical and fuel injection system of your engine, repair of turbochargers is best entrusted to specialists, apart from superficial cleaning of the blades of impellers and the inside of casings. Sometimes exchange assemblies are available for the impellers, but if not it should not be too difficult to replace them provided the assembly is carefully balanced afterwards.

nine

Cooling Systems

In an internal combustion engine the energy contained in each gallon of fuel is turned into heat, and approximately one-third of this is converted into useful work in the engine by turning the crankshaft, while about two-thirds of this heat is carried away, divided equally in the exhaust gases and in the cooling system (Fig 47). This means that if water be the coolant medium (although sometimes air is successfully used), a sufficient flow must be brought to the engine to keep the maximum temperatures internal and external from becoming unacceptably high. With an almost limitless supply of water around a boat one would imagine this task as being of no great magnitude. In practice, however, it is surprising that problems from the cooling system arise affecting the running and reliability of engines, and arise they do.

The three types of water cooling used in marine engines are by direct sea water, by keel pipes, and by fresh water and heat exchanger.

Direct Cooling

Direct cooling involves drawing water from the element in which the boat is floating, circulating it round the engine, and expelling it over the side again, often mixed with the exhaust gases. The main problems are ensuring an optimum coolant temperature, and secondly contamination of the water supply (with consequent deposits inside the engine).

Although thermostat control has been devised for direct cooled engines, its functioning is not always reliable. This is because internal passages in the engine and the thermostat itself are subjected to any dirt and other extraneous particles which may be picked up by the pump. This dirt may include a proportion of weed, mud and perhaps sand and salt. Thermostat settings are usually no higher than 135°F (57°C) to avoid salt deposition, which is less than ideal and there may be a tendency either to overcool or, at the opposite end of the scale, to overheat because of deliberate restriction at the sea water intake cock (Fig 48).

Periodical checks should be made on the whole system, and especially the cleaning of the sea water intake strainer which should be of adequate size with not too coarse a mesh, so that there is some chance of settling out entrained sand. Checking thermostats can be carried out by removing them and gradually heating them up in a container of water, noting the temperatures at which they crack open and are fully open. Most thermostats are of the fail-safe design so that if, on removing it, you find the thermostat cracked or wide open you will not need to test it to know that it needs replacing. Don't remove the thermostat and try to control water outlet temperature by screwing down the sea-cock. Removal of the thermostat may affect the by-pass, and thus the flow of available water to the vital parts of the engine will be reduced. If you have a wet exhaust, a reduced

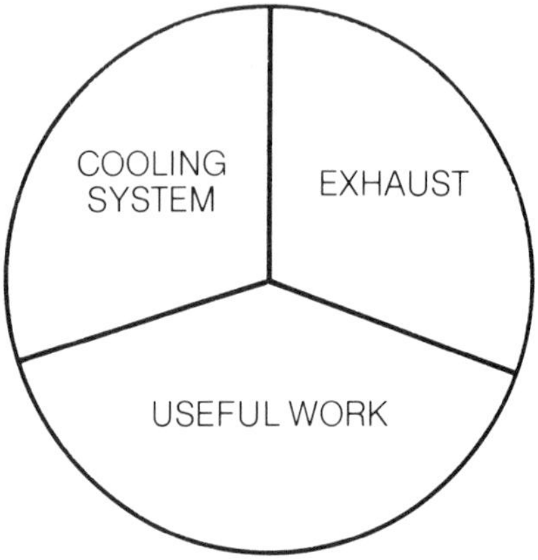

Fig 47. Diagram showing disposal of heat from the fuel of a diesel engine. Approximately one third of the heat energy from every gallon of fuel supplied has to be disposed of through the cooling system, rather more if the engine cooling water is also used to cool the exhaust.

flow risks overheating the exhaust pipe and may result in local overheating in the cylinder head, with possible cracking in the bottom deck of the head which you won't be able to see, or head gasket failure which you may be able to see.

Keel Cooling

This involves fresh water circulating in a closed circuit, part of which passes along pipes exposed to the cooling influence of the surrounding sea water along the keel area. It is a half-way house to full heat exchanger

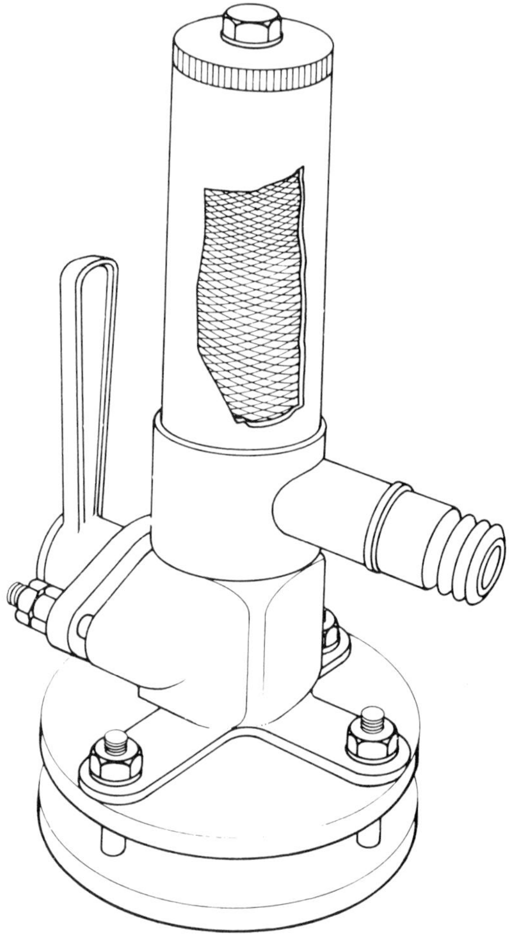

Fig 48. A seacock with seawater strainer combined.

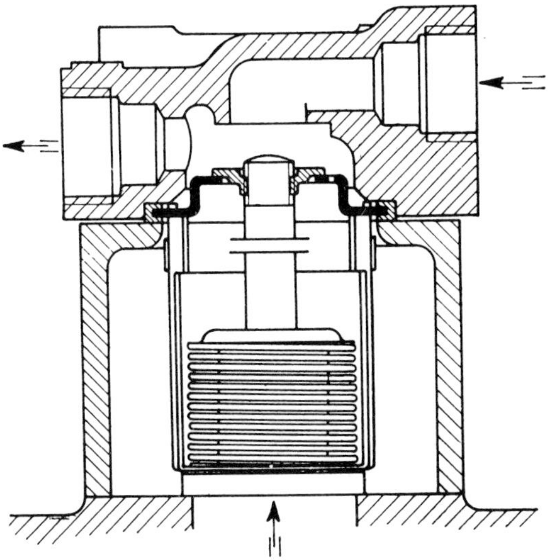

Fig 49. A bellows type thermostat as used on the Bukh engine with direct seawater cooling.

indirect cooling, but avoids some of the disadvantages of direct cooling (Fig 50).

It is unaffected by the cleanliness of the water in which the boat is floating but the outside cooling pipes may need mechanical cleaning from time to time, particularly if weed growth is heavy or barnacle formation on the bottom is prevalent in the area, in which case the boat will have to be slipped, sometimes more than once a season. A thermostat to maintain optimum operating temperature may be set higher than in the case of direct cooled engines, and this helps with reduced noise and smoke and improved efficiency. It is frequently set to start to open at 165°F (77°C). It should be checked for proper opening action as mentioned above. The correct setting temperature is usually stamped on the valve by the makers.

The header tank should be checked for level of coolant regularly and diesel antifreeze with a rust inhibitor may be used with this arrangement if required, otherwise distilled water is advisable. Once a year the skin fittings should be uncoupled from inside the boat and the keel pipes flushed out with a high pressure hose. This will not be necessary if copper pipes have been used because they do not rust, but is a useful practice nevertheless.

Any rubber hoses used for connections, particularly on the engine suction side of the water pump, must be examined periodically, preferably when the engine is running, to make sure that they show no signs of collapse; if they do, they must be replaced immediately; the replacement should be of the reinforced type. I have found that synthetic plastic pipes of heavy section are satisfactory in cold water.

Indirect Heat Exchanger Cooling

A heat exchanger operates on the same principle as a keel cooler, except that a special radiator is incorporated in the fresh water circuit instead of cooling pipes along the keel; this radiator is cooled by sea water

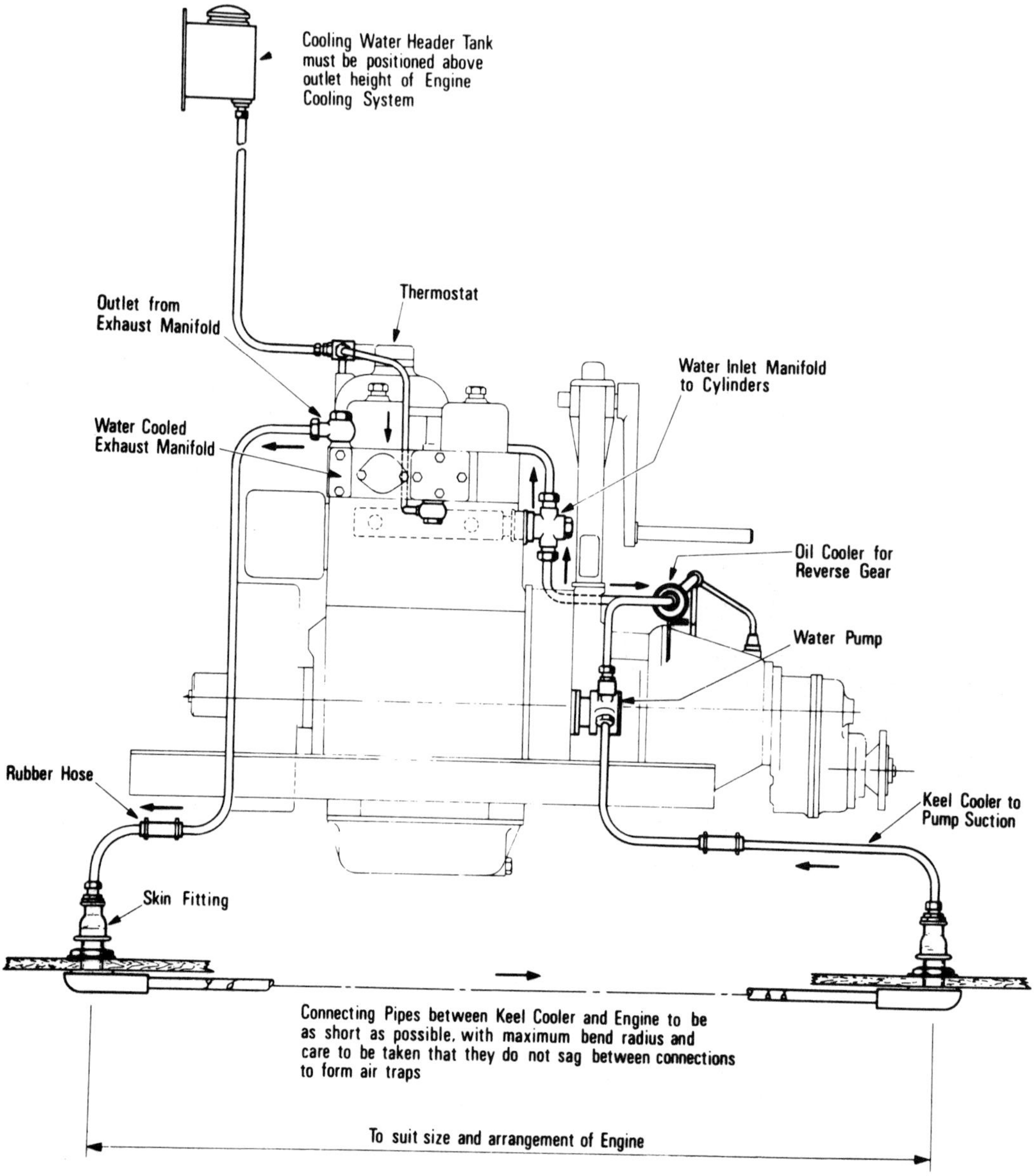

Fig 50. Schematic drawing of a keel cooling system (Petter).

Fig 51a. Removing seawater pump end plate.

pumped through it. The system uses two water pumps, one of which is for sea water which is drawn in through the bottom of the boat via the usual strainer combined with a sea cock; the latter can be closed when the engine is not running and the strainer removed for cleaning. The frequency of cleaning of suction strainers must be determined from experience because it depends on many variables, not least of which is the presence of weed and silt in the water, so that it is a good idea to start checking it daily until experience shows that the frequency can be relaxed. The second pump circulates the fresh water in its own closed system.

The advantage of keel cooling and of a heat exchanger is that sea water corrosion is reduced, and the water jacket temperature controlled at optimum for efficiency.

Sea Water Pump. The sea water pump is frequently of the rubber or neoprene impeller type (Fig 51 a and b). These have been found

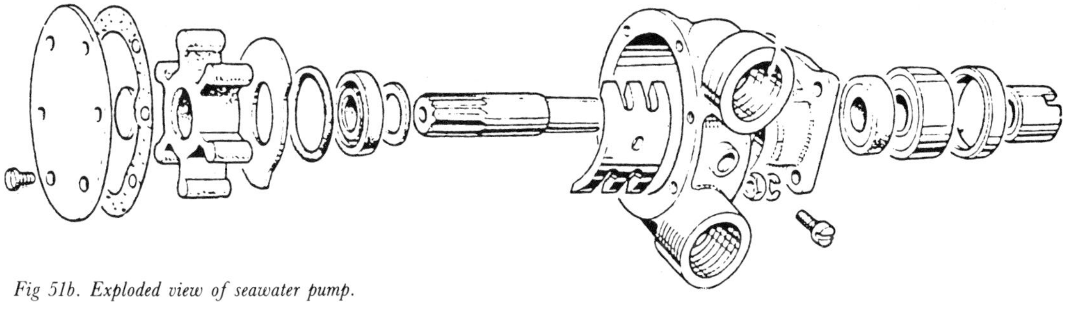

Fig 51b. Exploded view of seawater pump.

to tolerate a certain amount of dirt such as is normally found in sea water, but is should be inspected periodically for wear and for broken or cracked vanes. While it may continue to pump adequately with the odd vane missing, the missing piece can lodge in an outlet port and completely block the delivery of water. It is as well, therefore, to inspect the impeller at least once per season. When reassembling, a touch of grease will greatly assist in sliding the impeller into the pump body and prevent damage on first starting up dry. It is preferable to put the grease into the pump body rather than on the impeller. Always keep a spare impeller on board.

Sometimes the coolant is drawn in from the sea cock and strainer via the oil cooler for the gearbox, so that all water connections on the suction side of the water pump are below the level of the water line. This must be remembered when leaving the boat for any length of time on moorings, because all connections and hoses down there are potential sources of leak. The best way of avoiding trouble is of course to close the sea-cock after use, not a tiresome routine providing it is accessible, as it should be.

Coolers. Once the sea water has been drawn into the system it is available for the various tasks which may be required. Most manufacturers direct it through heat exchangers or coolers before finally discharging it overboard via the exhaust pipe. The first is the oil cooler (sometimes combined in a unit with the main heat exchanger). Typical units are illustrated in Fig 52. No maintenance is normally required for these components, apart from occasional cleaning of the tube stacks by means of a hose and checking of rubber sealing rings in the end plates. This certainly should not be necessary every season, but cleaning out may show up advance warning of corrosion in the tubes, and you will have to decide whether to take action before further trouble develops. If water mixes with the lubricating oil or vice versa a whole train of problems is liable to ensue.

Fresh Water Pump. The circulation of fresh water coolant around the engine and through the heat exchanger is usually performed by an automotive type pump with a centrifugal impeller driven by a V-belt from the crankshaft (Fig 53). These pumps require no servicing other than checking for rock or slop in the bearings. Bearings should last the overhaul life of the engine at which point a replacement or exchange unit pump should be considered. If, however, the non-adjustable seal should leak, then the bearings may suffer from some ingress of water and their life becomes suspect. The identification of such a problem becomes more simple if, when a new driving belt is fitted or the old belt is retensioned as part of routine servicing, the water pump pulley is felt by hand to have excessive play. In that event is should be inspected subsequently to make sure that the play has not become progressively worse

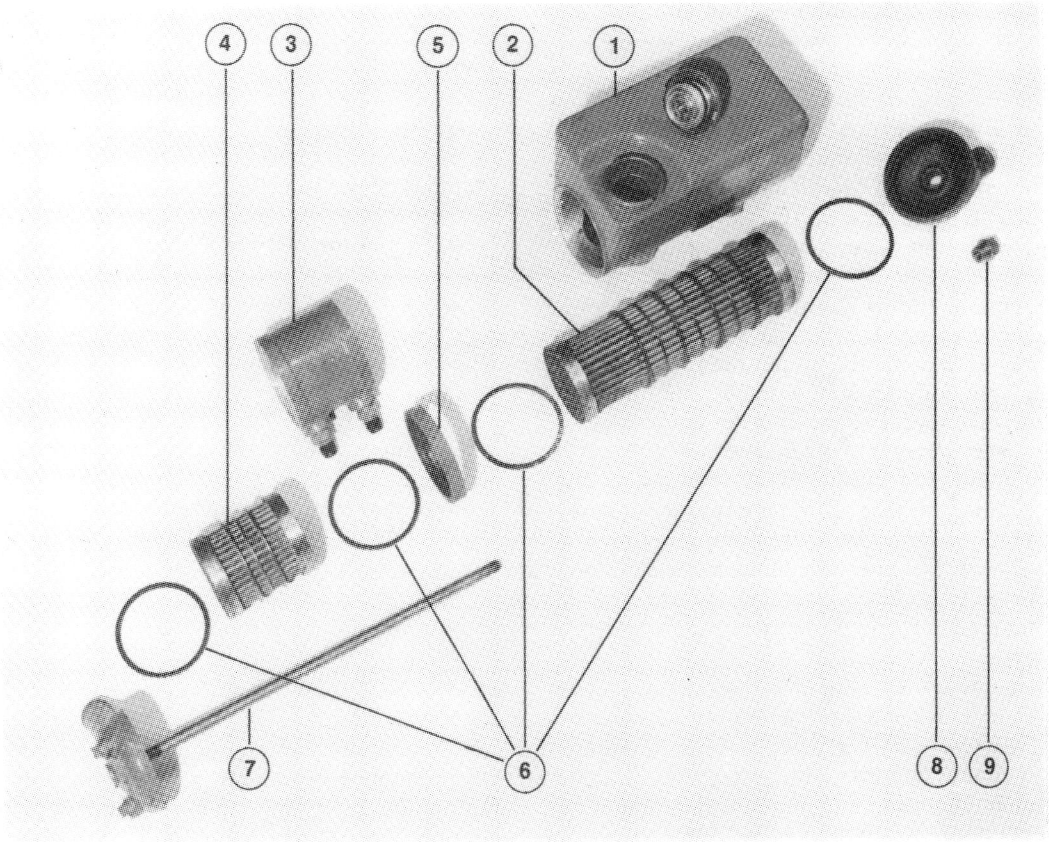

Fig 52. An oil cooler and a heat exchanger and header tank combined in one unit (Perkins 4.107).
1) Heat Exchanger Casing. 2) Tube Stack for Engine Coolant. 3) Oil Cooler Casing. 4) Tube Stack for Lubricating Oil. 5) Spacer. 6) 'O' Rings. 7) Tie Rod. 8) End Cover. 9) Cap Nut.

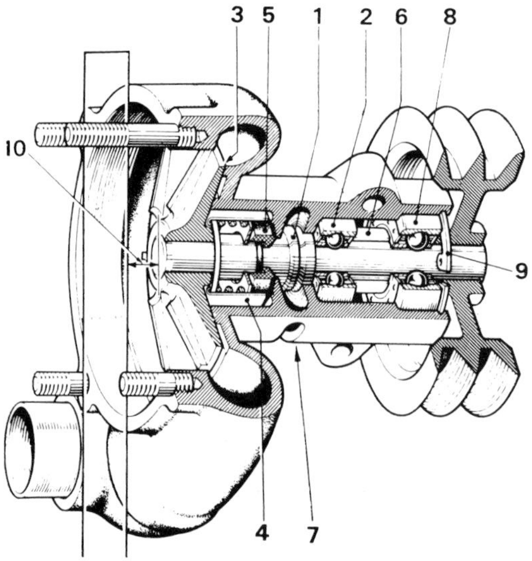

Fig 53. A typical heavy duty fresh water circulation pump (Lister).
1) Impeller Shaft. 2) Ball Bearing (small). 3) Impeller. 4) Carbon Ring Driver. 5) Carbon Ring. 6) Bearing Space. 7) Drain Hole in Pump Body. 8) Ball Bearing (large). 9) Circlip. 10) Clearance between impeller and cover needs to be checked.

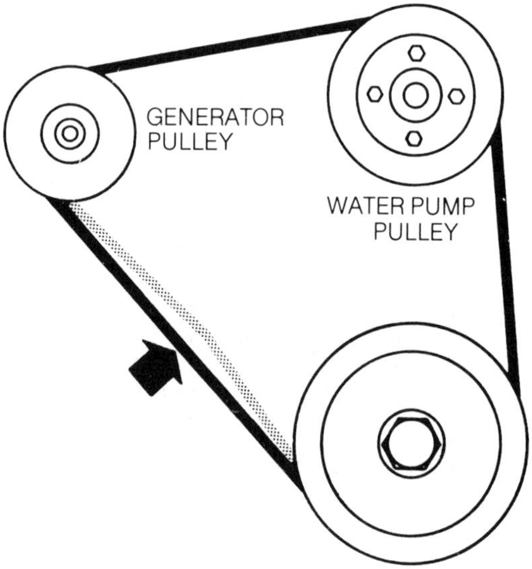

Fig 54. Regular checking the belt drive to fresh water pump and alternator is important. Deflection on the average should be about ½" when subject to thumb pressure at the point shown. Check with manufacturer's literature for any variation on this figure. Before tensioning the belt is the time to check the pump pulley for signs of rock.

or that there is no leak from the seal. If either is the case a service exchange pump is indicated (Fig 54).

Thermostat. In indirect cooling systems the thermostat is usually incorporated in the engine side or freshwater side of the system, so that it is not subjected to the sea water environment. It should be examined periodically though, unless there is a temperature gauge in the system. In this event it may be satisfactory to leave it until the engine is dismantled for overhaul, when it should be renewed, unless the temperature gauge shows abnormal readings in the meantime (Fig 55).

Pressure Caps. Header tanks are usually fitted with pressure caps, with the pressure setting

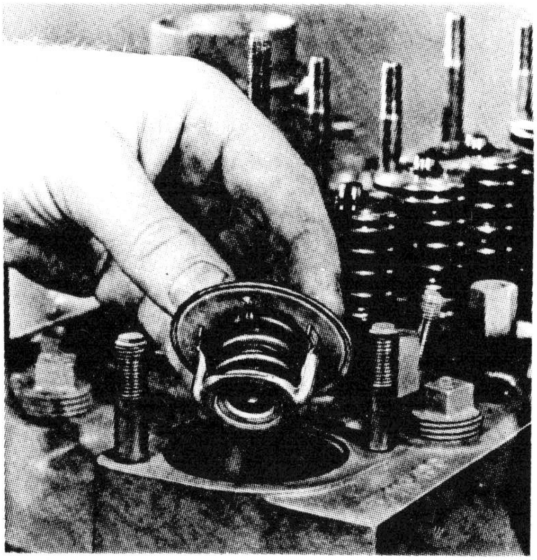

Fig 55. *Examining a thermostat. This one is of the wax capsule type, on a Perkins 4.107.*

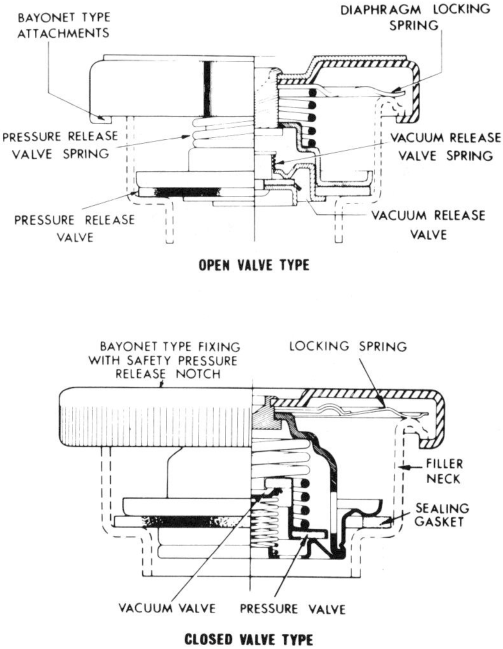

Fig 56. Header tank pressure relief caps; open (top) and closed (bottom) valve types. There are good technical reasons for using a pressurised system not least of which is the suppression of local boiling occurring in the hotter parts of the engine which can lead to coolant loss and undesirable deposits. Properly fitting and sealing pressure caps raise the boiling point of the coolant by approximately 2.8°F for every 1 lb increase in setting over atmospheric pressure. Thus a 10 lbf sq. in. pressure cap will increase the boiling point from 212°F (100°C) to 240°F (116°C). With a pressurised cooling system there is a need for watching for leaks in all connections particularly hoses and hose clips which should be the subject of a routine examination and replacement as necessary. In time hoses may tend to perish because of the higher pressures and temperatures. They may also tend to collapse on cooling if the small valve in the cap designed to release any vacuum should fail to work.

marked on the top in lb per sq in (Fig 56). The makers usually advise replacing these items in land service every year or so. Marine duties would seem not to be any more demanding, but the boat owner would be well advised to have them checked at the beginning of a new season. They can be tested quite simply by most larger service stations. If you have a leak at the pressure cap you will begin to suspect it by tell-tale marks on the header tank, especially if, as is advisable, the engine side of the cooling system has been treated with anti-freeze.

ten

Exhaust Systems

Over many years of experience of engines running in a wide variety of application and circumstance, I have learned that the performance of the best of them can be less than satisfactory or may even be ruined by indifferent installation. This is true of the inlet and exhaust systems in boats and, once an engine has been apparently satisfactorily installed and has passed trials run by boatbuilders, there is always the possibility of something deteriorating in use or actually going wrong. This possibility is much reduced if proper care was taken in installation and subsequent care is taken in service. There are two general types of exhaust system employed with small marine engines: the sea water cooled type, with or without a silencer, and the dry type. Most engine makers will give advice on both systems, with diagrams of typical recommended layouts, some of which are reproduced here.

Water Cooled Exhausts

Water cooled systems which are preferred for the majority of craft can have many variations. The important feature of water cooling is to ensure that the exhaust runs cool enough to be able to pass through enclosed areas of the boat without risk of fire. It should be accessible throughout its length from engine to stern, or to the side of the boat, whichever position has been chosen. The first indication of running dry of the essential cooling water is an altered exhaust note, most audible to the helmsman if the exhaust is taken out at the side. Usually a glance overboard immediately after starting up the engine and before leaving moorings will tell you that water is coming through, but regular inspection of the intake strainer should be undertaken, the frequency depending upon local circumstances and experience.

Connections. The connections in water cooled exhaust systems should be accessible for inspection regularly, because a corroded clip at a low point can lead to trouble; trouble from jamming of the clip itself at best, or at worst, should it corrode and become weakened, trouble from leakage.

I was once proceeding down an estuary to sea for a day's fishing when boat speed seemed to be dropping for no apparent reason. Then I noticed bilge water had risen to the level of the cockpit floor and we were somewhat low in the water. In a normally dry bilged boat something serious in the way of a leak must have developed. It transpired to be a split in the convoluted rubber exhaust hose not normally visible, and only detectable by feeling round to the underside where it formed a loop which had chafed and split in the lowest part of the bilge. The raw water coolant was being discharged into the inside of the boat. An immediate repair would not have been too difficult if the hose clips had not been rusted solid. As it was, the only casualty was a day's fishing due to a missed tide – but it might have been otherwise. On the credit side, an object lesson in maintenance which is passed on.

One of the other points worth checking occasionally is corrosion sometimes taking place around the flange of a light alloy injection bend, where it is bolted to the exhaust manifold. A light wire brushing and a coat of paint, preferably one of the anti-corrosion treatments with an undercoat to suit, will do much to keep it at bay.

Run-back. Most wet exhaust systems present some risk of sea water running back into the exhaust ports of the engine where it could cause damage. This risk is reduced to minimum by having a fall from the engine to the outlet just on or above the water line. This is often not possible with an engine installed low down in the boat, so that the pipe run to the outlet at least should be in a downwards direction as shown in Fig 57. The silencer if any should preferably be placed in the final downwards bend so that there is no fear of its filling up with water. The drain cock should be opened to drain water after running in frosty weather and closed again immediately all water has been drained.

Back Pressure. Some small engines used for auxiliaries are equipped with long absurdly narrow exhaust pipes which, when used in conjunction with water cooling, offer a lot of back pressure. This prevents the engines from developing their full power and will tend to make them smoke and be poor

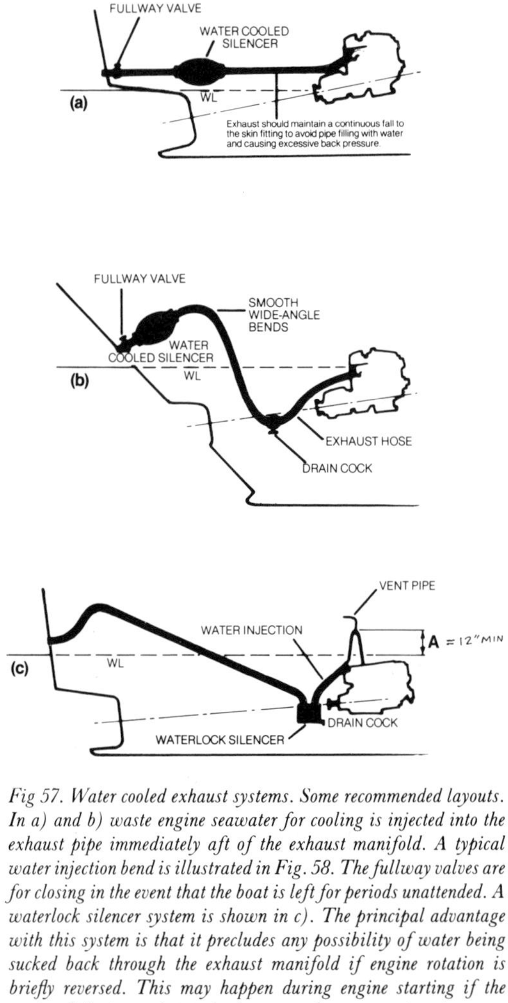

Fig 57. Water cooled exhaust systems. Some recommended layouts. In a) and b) waste engine seawater for cooling is injected into the exhaust pipe immediately aft of the exhaust manifold. A typical water injection bend is illustrated in Fig. 58. The fullway valves are for closing in the event that the boat is left for periods unattended. A waterlock silencer system is shown in c). The principal advantage with this system is that it precludes any possibility of water being sucked back through the exhaust manifold if engine rotation is briefly reversed. This may happen during engine starting if the engine fails to reach top dead centre when on compression.

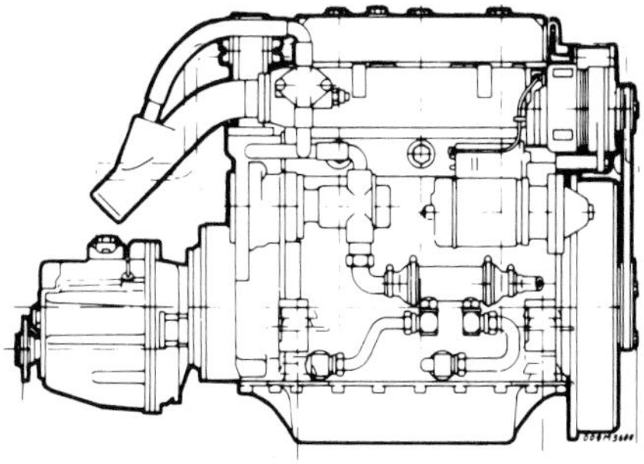

Fig 58. A drawing of a BUKH three cylinder engine which shows clearly the swan necked exhaust outlet bend with provision for water injection, avoiding run back into the engine.

starters. Limits for back pressure are available from makers of most engines, likewise recommendations for pipe sizes and lengths.

Dry Type Exhausts

The dry system is suitable for some boats, particularly open boats and those fitted with air cooled engines. It is often favoured by fishermen who tend to go for functional simplicity rather than refinement. Even with a silencer, the dry system tends to be less quiet than water cooled types in which the water itself acts to muffle the sound so that silencers are sometimes actually dispensed with.

Dry exhausts are commonly fitted vertically, connecting the exhaust manifold via a flexible metallic pipe and a bend which will collect rain water or condensation. There should be a drain cock at the lowest point of the bend, and this must be regularly opened to prevent any accumulation of water running back into the exhaust ports and cylinders. The general durability of such systems is liable to be somewhat less than a wet exhaust, and replacement of flexible pipes and other parts must be made when these deteriorate due to corrosion and leakage of exhaust fumes; even the odd spark from flange joints can present a fire hazard if these are neglected. I have seen vertical exhaust pipes with counterbalanced flaps on the outlets (borrowed from agricultural tractor practice), which is neater than the inverted tin can used by some fishermen to keep out the weather when the engine is left unused for some time; not a bad idea at all and much better than a rusted valve stem followed by a sticking valve.

eleven
Gearboxes and Transmissions

Most marine reversing gearboxes over recent decades have been produced with epicyclic gear trains, into which could be incorporated two of the most desirable features of a marine transmission:

1. the ability to change smoothly from ahead to astern by the operation of a single lever;
2. the ability to provide full power and shaft speed ahead or astern, thus affording maximum manoeuvrability.

Well-known makes of transmission have been designed around the epicyclic principle, first mass produced in the automotive field in the model 'T' Ford car. This may have been one of the reasons why those engines were a popular choice for marine conversions. They did suffer, however, from the wrong speed ratio in reverse: right for automobiles but hopelessly slow for marine purposes, being ineffective both in capacity to slow down the boat and in providing adequate propulsion astern against a tide. They possessed the advantage of being in constant mesh astern, operable by a clutch, which all other car boxes did not, because these needed a separate clutch and gear shift lever.

Manufacturers of marine engines used the epicyclic principle, and either made their own boxes or employed proprietary reverse gears, of which there have been many. They were sometimes cumbersome additions to the already rather heavy engines of the time and, although the reversing process was achieved by a single control, operation was slow. The introduction of hydraulic clutches has made the helmsman's task simpler and lighter.

Adjustment of Epicyclic Boxes

On the whole epicyclic boxes have been trouble-free, requiring little maintenance, with only two provisos: the first being regular adjustment of ahead and astern clutches, and the second the provision of clean and adequate lubrication. Frequency and adjustment of clutches depends on use. A fishing boat or work boat engine spends a relatively high proportion of its life in rapid changes of power output, inching ahead and astern, and this involves wear of clutches and gears, whereas a pleasure yacht auxiliary engine does not have anything like the rough use. The important thing to remember is that no clutches like being deliberately slipped with too wide a throttle opening. When such demands are made, as in an emergency, it is doubtful whether more rapid stopping can be achieved in this way. The actual adjustment of ahead and astern clutches varies with different makes, but can usually be achieved by loosening and retightening nuts as detailed in the maker's instruction book. Sometimes special tools are desirable to simplify the procedure, which is usually carried out after removal of inspection covers (Figs 59 and 60).

It is a good idea to study the action of the box while on moorings with the engine at low throttle; remove the appropriate floor boards

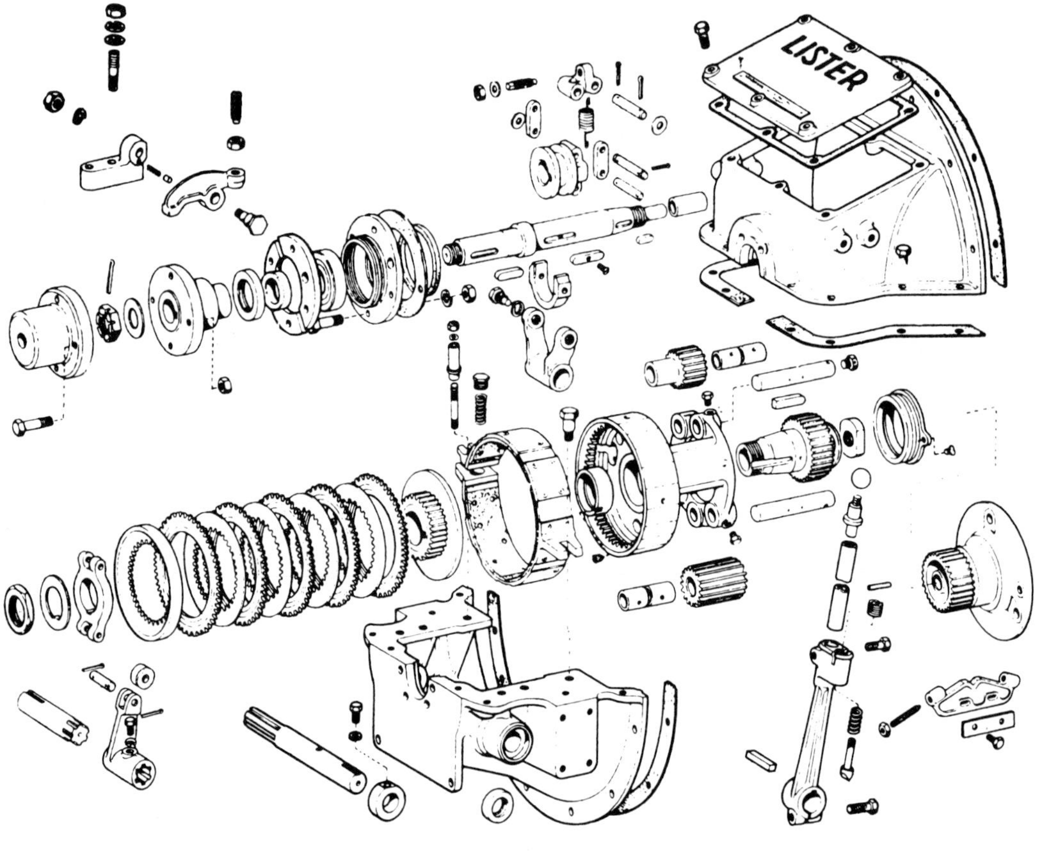

Fig 59. An exploded view of a Lister 39 epicyclic gearbox. Showing the multiplate ahead gear clutch and the hand brake clutch for reverse.

Fig 60. Adjusting points for Lister 39 clutches.
A) Sliding sleeve. B) Toggle lever screws. C) Brake band lever adjusting screw.

if necessary so that the inboard end of the propeller shaft can be seen. In this way the engagement of the clutches can be checked and also the action of the remote controls when fitted. A good clean engagement should occur, together with a positive dwell period in neutral corresponding to the neutral position indicated on the control. With epicyclic boxes, especially those with multi-plate clutches, there may be some creep in neutral; this is mainly due to oil drag and, if it can be stopped by hand pressure on the shaft, it is nothing to cause concern. This check should be carried out by the inexperienced with special care, using a suitable piece of wood rather than the hand because of the inherent risk in handling a moving shaft.

Anybody who works regularly with machinery will be only too aware of the dangers of working in the vicinity of moving parts.

Having established that a positive neutral has been achieved, the only other thing that remains is to carry out trials under way, to check that the clutches do not slip. Short of removing the engine and having a dynamometer test carried out ashore, the only means open to the owner is a boat test at full speed. If adjustment has been properly carried out to maker's instructions this may be somewhat academic, but it is worth checking when next the opportunity occurs because there is nothing more true than the old adage 'the proof of the pudding is in the eating'.

Other Types of Gearbox

There has been a marked trend towards using a two-shaft gearbox, with the output shaft driven by normal spur gears from the input shaft situated above it. This leads to a somewhat simpler design with fewer moving parts than the epicyclic box. One of the objections to this type of drive in early versions was its bulk, but this seems to have been overcome with the use of improved design and materials permitting smaller dimensions all round (Fig 61).

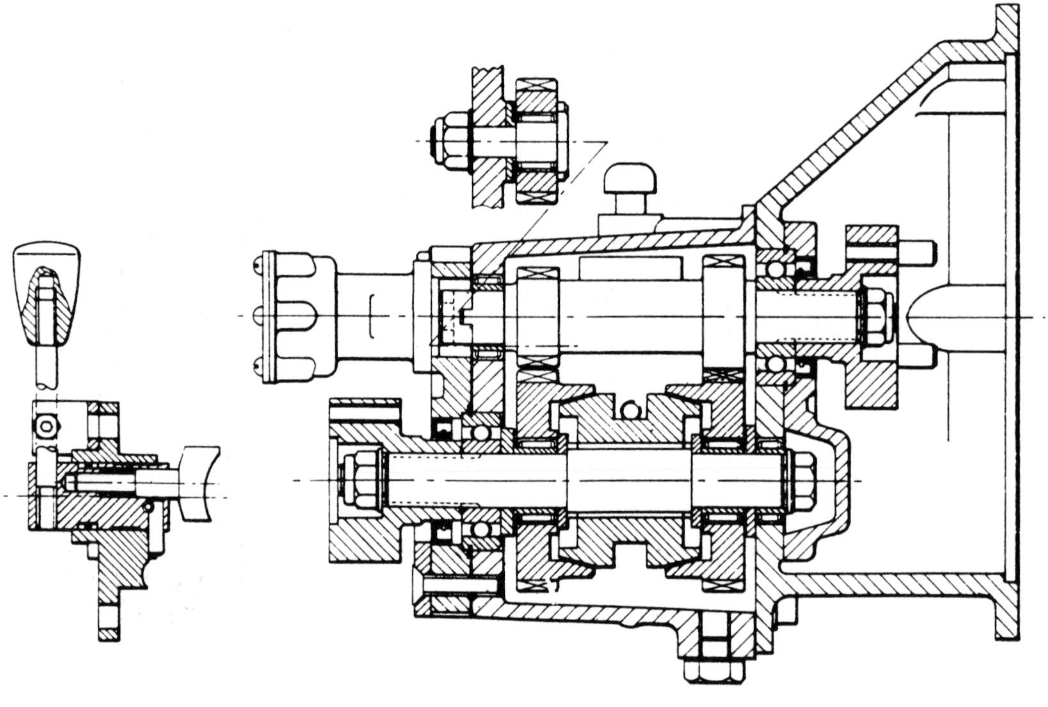

Fig 61. Cross-section of a two-shaft reverse and reduction box for a small engine, Stuart Sole Mk. II.

Fig 62. A German Hurth reverse and reduction box type HBW50 with manual operation.

An example of one of the Hurth range of boxes is shown, models of which are made from 2 to 280 kW. The power losses are somewhat less than the equivalent epicyclic boxes, and all have an optional built-in reduction ratio of between 1.5 and 2.7 to 1. Where oil temperatures are likely to exceed 270°F (130°C), oil cooling is advised (Fig 62).

Fig 63. An hydraulically operated Borg Warner Velvet Drive Model CR2 reverse and reduction gear, shown fitted to a Lister engine. Note the oil pipes leading to the gearbox oil cooler mounted across the top of the box. Also shown is the permanently fitted hand pump for oil drainage purposes. The small operating lever for the box is just visible on the far side.

Maintenance

Maintenance requirements of most modern gearboxes should include ensuring that there are no oil leaks and that the oil level is maintained. Gearbox oil should not need changing frequently since it does not become contaminated by combustion products as in the case of the engine, but it does have to contain the normal wear products of the gears, bushes and clutch plates. Filters where fitted should have their elements changed along with the oil at manufacturer's recommended intervals.

Breathers, which are usually fitted on the top of the casing, should be kept free from obstruction, and the entry of dirt and water either through the breathers or when filling with oil must be carefully avoided; dirt can play havoc with metal-to-metal clutch plates. Keeping clutches and controls in proper adjustment will ensure minimum slippage and obviate overheating and its consequent evils.

With most designs of reverse gearbox, lubricating and clutch oil under pressure is provided by a self-contained pump located within the casing and not usually accessible from outside the box. Oil operated clutches avoid the need for mechanical levers within the box, and control is effected from an hydraulic valve usually situated externally and requiring little mechanical effort. There is normally a relief valve which can be adjusted if necessary, but this should not be

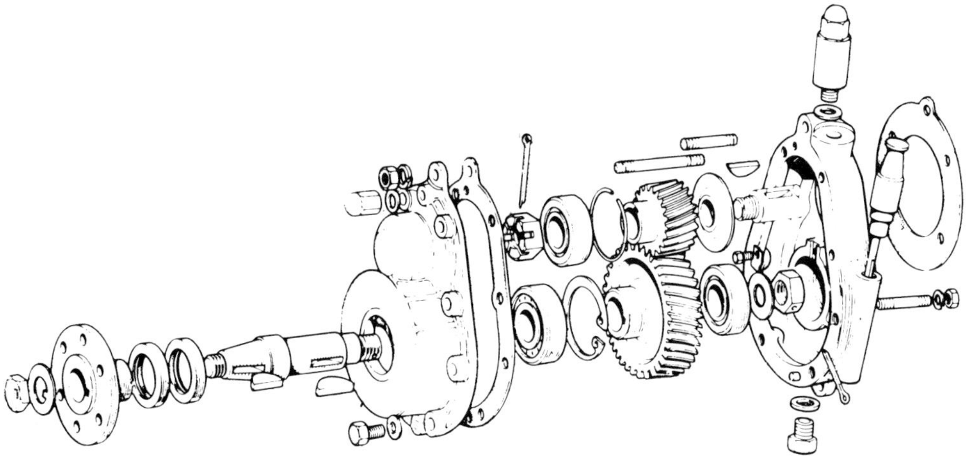

Fig 64. Exploded view of a Lister reduction box. This has as an added precaution against leaks two seals on the output shaft, the inner one for oil and the outer one to prevent seawater from the bilges gaining access. To be seen on the right are the dipstick for checking oil level and the combined filler breather at the top of the casing

considered unless the makers advise it. In fact most makers do not even install an oil pressure gauge, and the relief valve will only require resetting after complete overhaul of the box. Most troubles in reverse boxes fall within one of three categories.

1. Overheating, due to excessive clutch slip.
2. Water or dirt in the box.
3. Incorrect adjustment of remote control mechanism.

Adjustment of controls is something which should be checked at least once a season and in any case after adjustment of clutches on the gearbox. The trend today is towards remote controls by flexible cables remote from the engine. The important feature to be checked is that from 'full ahead' to 'full astern' the movement on the gearbox lever faithfully follows the movement at the control position. Likewise that, when in the 'neutral' position on the gearbox, the position of the control exactly corresponds. The throttle, when interlinked in a single lever control, should also be checked for full travel with neutral position corresponding to a fully closed throttle.

Reduction Gears

Other frequently fitted transmissions are the Borg Warner, which is shown in Fig 63, and which can be equipped with a reduction gear or not as required. In direct drive version it is ideally suited to high-speed light weight engines in planing craft driving small propellers, but it is equally at home turning large propellers through integral reduction boxes. This box has a deserved reputation for reliability and requires little maintenance. The makers supply spare parts made up in the form of kits, which are helpful because they anticipate, as a result of experience, what may most be needed for overhauls.

Reduction gearboxes are usually designed to run to the major overhaul life of the engine before attention is required. When it is required it will probably include replacement of bearings, usually on the output side if it has been running or standing in bilge water, and of the oil seals (Fig 64). A small polished line on the output coupling boss will show if there has been good contact with seals but, if this line is pitted with patches of rust you can be sure the seal has been leaking and the bearing must be examined for wear, and bearings, shaft seals and output coupling should be replaced. The coupling can sometimes be saved by moving its position axially in relation to the seal, so that the mating lip of the seal operates on a fresh, unworn surface of metal. If the seal itself cannot be repositioned it will be necessary to fit a washer or distance piece of no more than ⅛ in thickness to reposition the coupling. This small axial displacement in the propeller shaft can usually be tolerated. The above procedure cannot be adopted in the case of the Lister reduction box illustrated, because the output coupling is fitted on a taper which fixes its axial position.

twelve
The Electrical System

In big ships there is usually at least one Engineer Officer whose responsibilities may be almost entirely concerned with the maintenance and repair of electrical equipment. In sustaining the life and proper functioning of all departments of the ship, this work has become more and more complicated. In private yachts and small boats the owner/ skipper finds himself a student of seamanship, then a practical rigger, then a navigator, and last but not least a would-be engineer with a working knowledge of diesels. Knowledge of electricity is often not regarded as a *sine qua non* of the boating man's qualifications, but at least a 'what-for and why' of electrical equipment must be included in that knowledge, if only to enable him to understand the basic principles of care and maintenance of it.

Get to Know your Installation

While diesels will *run* perfectly satisfactorily without electrics, there is the question of *starting*, which is usually best resolved by the use of electricity, thus involving the use of batteries — which have to be charged — and so on. In fact the need for electricity on board stems from three quite different but interlinked requirements.

1. Starting the engine
2. Lighting the boat, inside and outside
3. Auxiliaries, domestic and navigational

The requirements may be conflicting and, in order to exercise some economy, the choice of equipment to avoid unnecessary duplication and first cost calls for some expertise (Fig 65).

Starter Motors

There are two main types of starter motor used in small marine diesels, the difference being in the method of drive and engagement with the engine flywheel gear ring. The first is the inertia drive starter, in which the pinion is mounted on a screwed sleeve or helix and the inertia of the pinion causes it to move along the helix into engagement with the flywheel ring as the motor accelerates. When the starter switch is released and it slows down, the pinion moves back out of engagement. The shock of initial engagement is taken through a substantial spring mounted on the end of the starter spindle (Fig 66).

The second type of starter, which is known as the pre-engaged type, is designed to prevent the pinion being prematurely thrown out of engagement when the engine first fires weakly or intermittently. This is achieved by current passing through a solenoid (which is combined with the starter) which, when energised, pulls a lever that moves the pinion into engagement with the flywheel. Not until the pinion is fully engaged will full current be allowed to flow through the starter itself (Fig 67).

Both types of starter are operated electrically by means of a separate solenoid switch

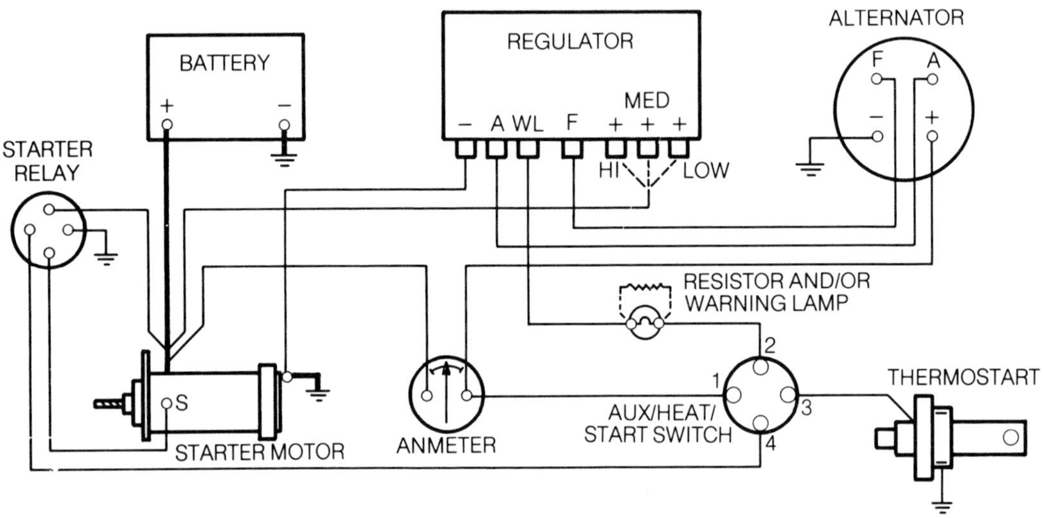

Fig 65. A typical electrical circuit diagram.

which is energised by turning the low current key or switch, usually combined with the pre-heater switch, at the helmsman's position. This energises the primary winding of the solenoid whose contacts carry the high current of the starter. By mounting the solenoid on the engine itself the starter leads can be kept as short as possible.

Electrical care and maintenance of all the foregoing is limited to ensuring that cable connections are fully secure and free from corrosion. Mechanical maintenance for the inertia drive starter is confined to the drive end itself. The pinion should be examined for bruised teeth and freedom on the helical sleeve, which sometimes may become sluggish because of accumulations of dirt and rust which have been picked up within the flywheel housing. The application of a few drops of light oil is permissible, but grease should be avoided because this may tend to cause sticking.

The starter solenoid may become erratic or sluggish in action over a long period of time

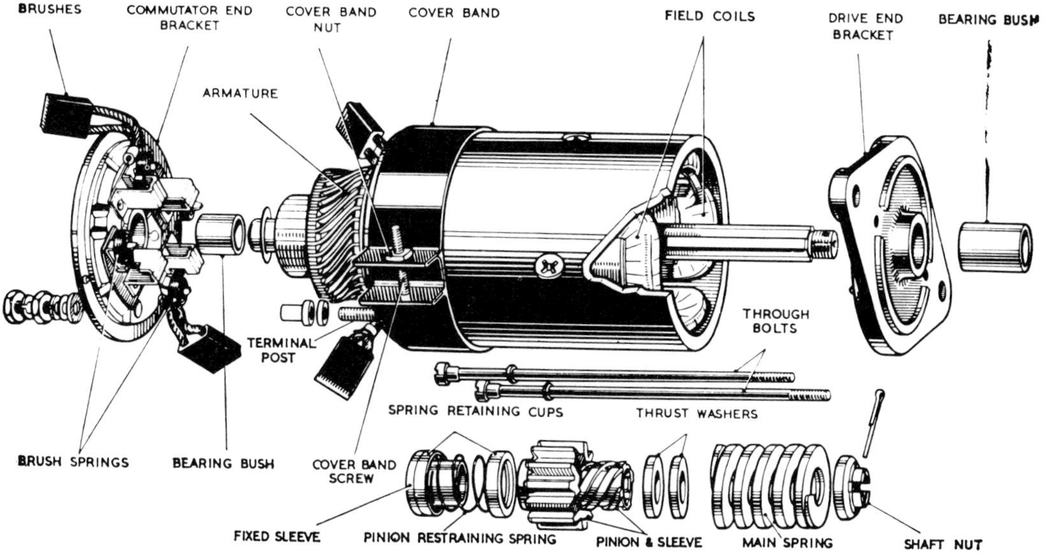

Fig 66. An inertia drive (Bendix) starter motor dismantled.

and fail to make proper contact. If it fails to work after making sure all electrical connections to it are good, fitment of a new unit is indicated. It is a good plan to include a spare starter solenoid unit in the boat's kit.

The brushes and commutator in the starter should be given attention in the same way as for dynamos, dealt with later in this chapter.

Cold Starting Aids

In focusing our attention on starting, the important thing to remember is that a diesel will always start more quickly if it is cranked fast, and this depends on having a battery which gives a good voltage over the period of cranking. In cold weather the duration of cranking, and hence the drain on the battery, can be reduced appreciably by using one of the auxiliary starting aids available. Most engines are provided by their makers with one or more of these, and it is important that they should be used in accordance with the recommendations given for starting procedure. Study the instructions so that following them becomes second nature and you will

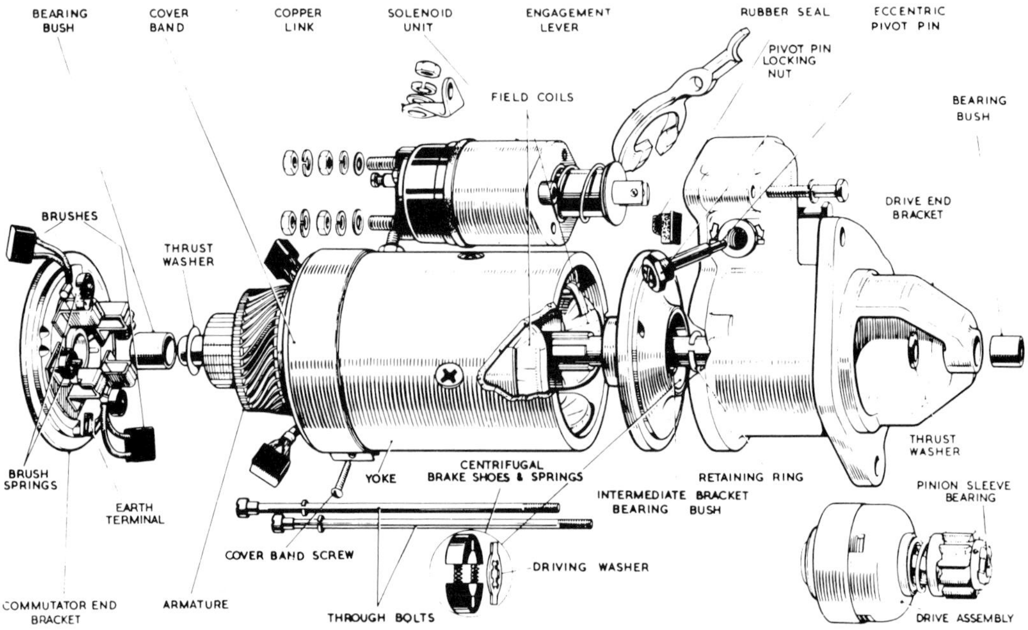

Fig 67. A pre-engaged starter motor dismantled.

save yourself a lot of trouble and grief.

The most commonly used aid fitted in the intake duct of many makes and types of engine is the Lucas/CAV Thermostart. This device, which should require little or no maintenance beyond seeing that it is supplied with fuel, has been developed after a great deal of practical experience in starting many types of diesel, but it needs to be used correctly. A pre-heating time of about 15 seconds is usual (see Fig 68).

Other aids to starting are electrical glow plugs fitted in individual cylinders or combustion chambers of indirect injection engines. These usually require a pre-heating time of as much as 30 seconds. They are of

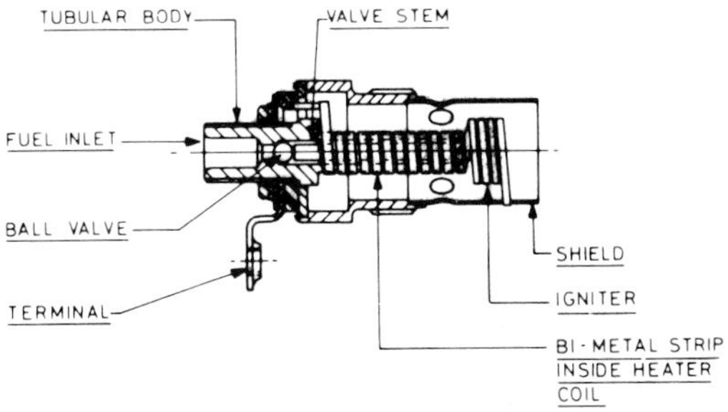

Fig 68. CAV Thermostart. This device is fed with fuel from the low pressure leak off system from the injectors, see also Fig. 25. It consists of an electrically controlled ball valve which opens under the influence of a bi-metal strip which heats up when a current is passed through the heater coil. One end of the coil is attached to the finer wire of the igniter which glows sufficiently to ignite the fuel already vaporised. When the engine starter is engaged the burning fuel is drawn out in a flame like a blow lamp, warming the remaining air in the manifold as it enters the individual cylinders. The valve closes as soon as the current is switched off when the engine is running. A combined switch for this heater and the starter motor facilitates the whole operation.

higher first cost than any of the other aids available and probably are marginally less reliable. For very cold climates the use of ether injected into the intake by a special applicator bolted to the manifold is common practice. More recently the practice of applying ether to the intake from a hand-held aerosol canister has become fairly widespread and, while this can be quite effective, it has a number of drawbacks, not least of which are on the grounds of safety in use and storage, and the possible ill effects on the engine of prolonged or incorrect use. Care must be taken to avoid squirting too much ether into the intake, and experience will very quickly indicate the correct amount. If the engine knocks badly during the cranking process, too much ether has been used. It must be repeated that abuse of ether can only do harm to the engine, sometimes expensive, and in any case will fail to assist in the starting process.

Starter Battery

All three of the requirements on the boat listed in the second paragraph of this chapter usually have to be met by one source of electrical power: the battery. It is essential, therefore, that this be adequate for its purposes throughout its life, which might be something like five years, sometimes more, before replacement. Over the years, unseen by the owner, battery efficiency will gradually deteriorate, and extra lights or equipment may have been added to the boat which contribute to the electrical demand upon it.

The power drain from the battery for starting your engine can be very high but, provided the engine is in good order, the actual period of time that this power is needed is brief. For example, a first start in cold weather without one of the aids already described might need the starter motor to turn the engine over for as long as 30 seconds. But this occurs only once per day, thereafter restarting a warm engine might take as little as 2 seconds. The battery thus has to be capable of delivering enough energy for the worst climatic conditions in which the boat is likely to be used. The current drawn from a 12-volt battery may be as high as 1,000 amps for the momentary breakaway torque of a cold engine, followed by 500 amps for up to 30 seconds before the engine finally runs, so that any aid to rapid starting will be beneficial.

The type and construction of battery capable of giving the best starting performance under very cold conditions is not always the best for lighting, etc, and so it is most important to see that the cold starting needs are first properly met. Most probably it will be found that the lighting and other requirements will also have been met, but not always, and that is why it is necessary to do a few sums if you want to check that all the electrical needs of your boat have been properly satisfied. Separate batteries for the lighting and auxiliaries may have been installed in the boat. These may be charged from the same alternator on the main engine or from a separate generator set, and where space is not at a premium, there is much to be said in favour of the latter arrangement. The reader who is considering rewiring his boat is recommended to refer to *Marine Electrical Systems* published by Lucas Marine or to *Electrics and Electronics for Small Craft* published by Adlard Coles Ltd.

Alkaline Batteries

The use of more costly alkaline (nickel-iron or nickel-cadmium) batteries has certain advantages, particularly in larger boats where separate sources are used for starting and lighting, the alkaline battery being reserved for starting purposes. Among the advantages over the conventional lead acid battery are those of a long life and a certain tolerance to neglect. However, and this again is where the influence of automotive practice is apparent, the use of lower-cost lead acid batteries is almost universal in small boats and hence these will be dealt with in more detail.

From the above it will be seen that some compromise will be involved in selecting a single suitable battery. But make no mistake, if one day you can't get the engine going because the starter won't shift it, unless your mooring is close to a local service station you are unlikely to go to sea that day.

Starter motor batteries must be maintained in good condition, not only to ensure effective use but also to protect the starter motor from overload – a point that is not generally realised but is nevertheless important. For example, if the terminal voltage applied to the starter is low, then slow cranking occurs with excessively high current flow in the motor, a process calculated to shorten the starter motor life and greatly increase service costs.

Lead Acid Batteries

Conventional lead acid batteries require to be charged regularly and must not be neglected during laying-up time. They slowly lose charge while standing, and the warmer the conditions of storage the greater the loss. At 65°F (18°C) the loss is approximately 1 per cent per day and at 100°F (38°C) it is approximately 3 per cent. If the battery is uncharged for periods of two to three months, self-discharge losses will result in sulphation of the plates thereby reducing efficiency.

Capacity. The capacity of a lead acid battery is related to its rate of discharge and is normally expressed in terms of a 10 hour rating. This means that a 250 amp hr battery at the 10 hour rate will supply 25 ampères for 10 hours when fully charged. The capacity of the same 250 amp hr battery will be reduced at a higher rate of discharge, e.g. at a two hour rating only 60 per cent (150 amp hr) of the rated capacity will be available.

Some idea of size of suitable capacity of batteries can be judged from a typical case. For starting purposes under normal climatic conditions, the popular Perkins 4.107/4.108 marine unit of 1.76 litres (107 cu in) swept volume needs a battery of 13 plates of a capacity of 76 ampère hours at the 10 hour rate. For commercial duties, a battery having 17 plates and capacity of 103 ampère hours at the 10 hour rate is recommended. Lucas suggest that a battery of 140 ampère hours capacity would be suitable for a small craft's average needs, including starting a 2–3 litre (120–180 cu in) engine.

A check of a conventional battery's condition, as opposed to its state of charge, may be obtained by using a suitable high-rate discharge tester, the prongs of which are applied to each 2 volt cell in turn. A cell in good condition will maintain a steady voltage for 10 seconds, whereas a rapidly falling voltage indicates a weak cell. To obtain accurate test figures the battery must be at least 70 per cent charged, and it is not recommended to use a high discharge tester whilst charging is in progress owing to the danger of spark-induced explosion of the hydrogen emitted from the cells. Topping up, preferably with clean distilled or de-ionised water should be carried out whenever necessary, so that there is always approximately ¼ in of electrolyte visible above the top of the plates. If the plates are allowed to become dry they will deteriorate and the battery will lose capacity. The battery's state of charge is determined by measuring the specific gravity of the electrolyte with a hydrometer. Average readings are:

1.280	Fully charged	taken at 60°F (16°C)
1.200	Half discharged	
1.115	Fully discharged	

Maintenance-free Batteries

The development of the so-called maintenance-free battery for automotive purposes in the United States promises to make an impact in the marine equipment field. Originally made by Delco, a subsidiary of General Motors, it is marketed in Europe by AC-Delco under the name Freedom and by Van Ouden under the trade name Vetus. Other battery manufacturers have been cautious in investing in the techniques of manufacture involved, but look like doing so.

The principal advantageous features of this new lead acid battery over the long established types, which use lead/antimony plates in a bakelite casing, are its plates made of lead/calcium enclosed within a polypropylene casing. This results in reduced gassing on charging, with consequent minimal losses of electrolyte and reduced weight and size. Other advantages are claimed by the makers which all contribute towards minimum maintenance and long life. This could obviate the need for the most costly nickel alkaline battery.

Cables and Connections

Remembering that the only source of electricity on your boat when the generator is not running is the battery, which for weight, size and reasons of cost is usually kept as small as possible consistent with performing its required function, it behoves the owner to ensure that the minimum waste of available power takes place. This is done by ensuring, first that the voltage drop in the cables and connections is minimal, and secondly that the leakage of current from all sources is minimised.

The most common mistake in installations is the provision of either too long cables for the starter, or cables of too small cross section which will tend to heat up and waste energy; the maximum resistance in the cables should not exceed 0.0017 ohm. A rough guide is that the cables must not exceed total (combined) length of 20 feet of minimum size 61/.044 (i.e. 61 strands of 0.044 in sectional area). Another common fault is poor connections from the battery and on the starter motor and solenoid, which must be clean and firm and kept free from corrosion. After you have started your diesel one day from cold, put your finger on each of the terminal connections all the way from the battery to the starter motor. If you burn your finger you will know which needs attention, but they all get hot and lose electrical energy in the process.

Battery Charging

Generation of electric current for charging batteries can be by means of the old-established automotive type dynamo or the more recent alternator.

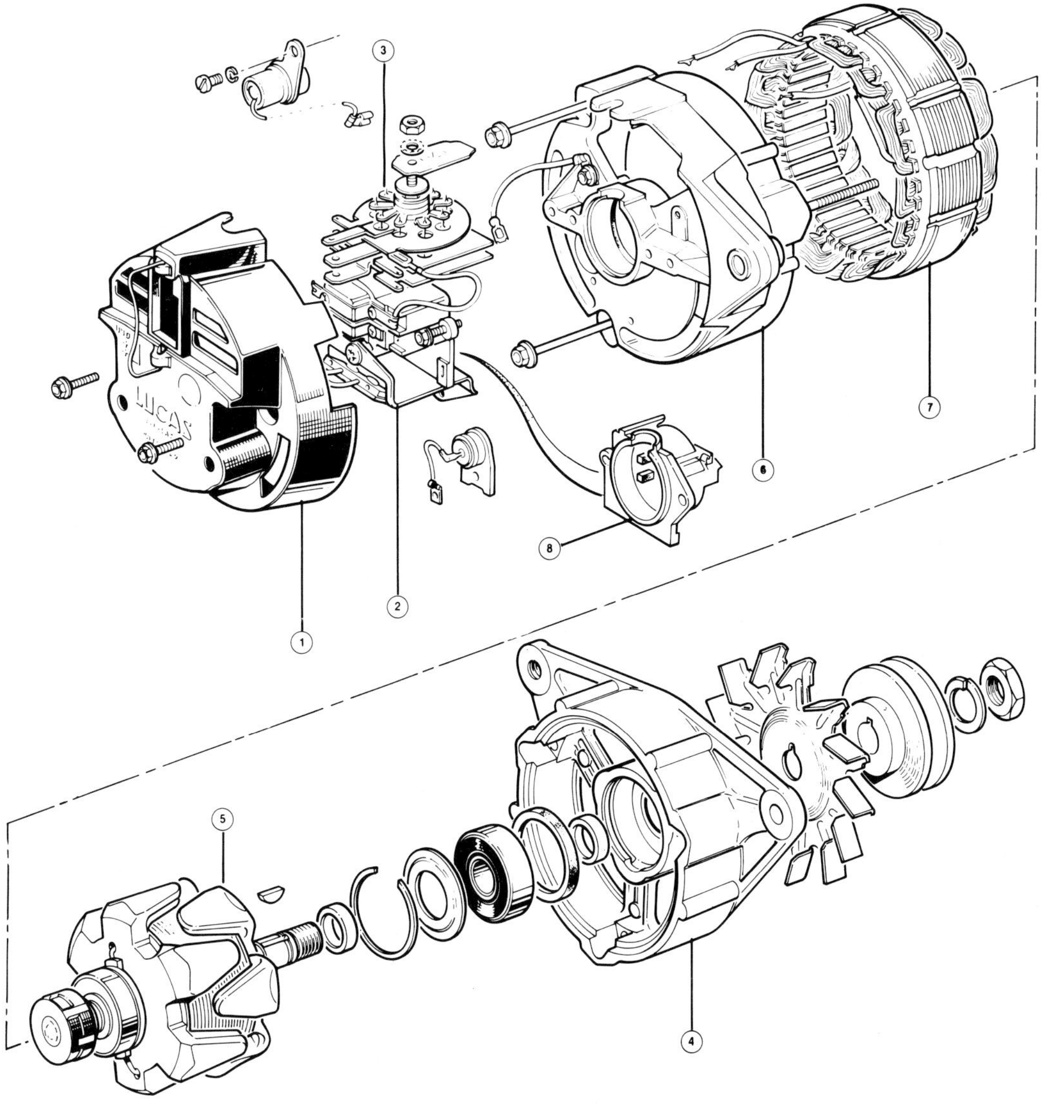

Fig 69. A typical alternator.
1) Cover. 2) Regulator. 3) Rectifier. 4) Bracket, drive end. 5) Rotor assembly. 6) Bracket, slip ring end. 7) Stator. 8) Brush box assembly.

Alternators

The most notable advantage of alternators is that, size for size, they are capable of providing a much higher output than dynamos both at low and high engine speeds, and they require practically no maintenance. Brush and slip ring wear is normally low, and these parts require even less attention than the corresponding ones in the dynamo. Although the alternator produces alternating current (AC), in modern machines it is converted to DC by means of a built-in rectifier pack which requires no attention. It does suffer from a major disadvantage of complete failure if the current should be cut off accidentally, for example by turning off the battery master switch while the engine is running, or if polarity is reversed for any reason, and certain safety rules must be observed.

The diodes in the alternator function as one-way valves and the transistors in the regulator/control box operate as fast switches. Both are accurate and sensitive. They do not wear out and seldom require adjustment but, because they are sensitive to voltage changes and high temperature, precautions are vital to prevent them from being destroyed. Therefore:

(a) DO NOT disconnect the battery whilst the engine is running. This will cause a voltage surge in the alternator charging system which will immediately ruin the diodes or transistors.

(b) DO NOT disconnect a lead without first stopping the engine and turning all electrical switches to the 'off' position.

(c) DO NOT cause a short circuit by connecting leads to incorrect terminals. Always identify a lead to its correct terminal. A short circuit or wrong connection giving reverse polarity will immediately and permanently ruin transistors or diodes.

(d) DO NOT connect a battery into the system without checking for correct polarity and voltage.

(e) DO NOT 'flash' connections to check for current flow. No matter how brief the contact the transistors may be ruined.

Suppression for Radio. Alternator charging systems may cause radio interference due to rapid switching action of transistors, and the abrupt cut-off of reverse currents by diodes. The interference generated by alternator and regulator is transmitted to radio receiving equipment either by radiation or by conduction. Interference is likely to prove more of a problem on larger craft fitted with medium frequency radio, and less or not at all with craft fitted with VHF only. When it occurs, the only effective remedy is to adopt fully screened electrical equipment on the engine. This may not always provide a complete answer, as some sources of interference may

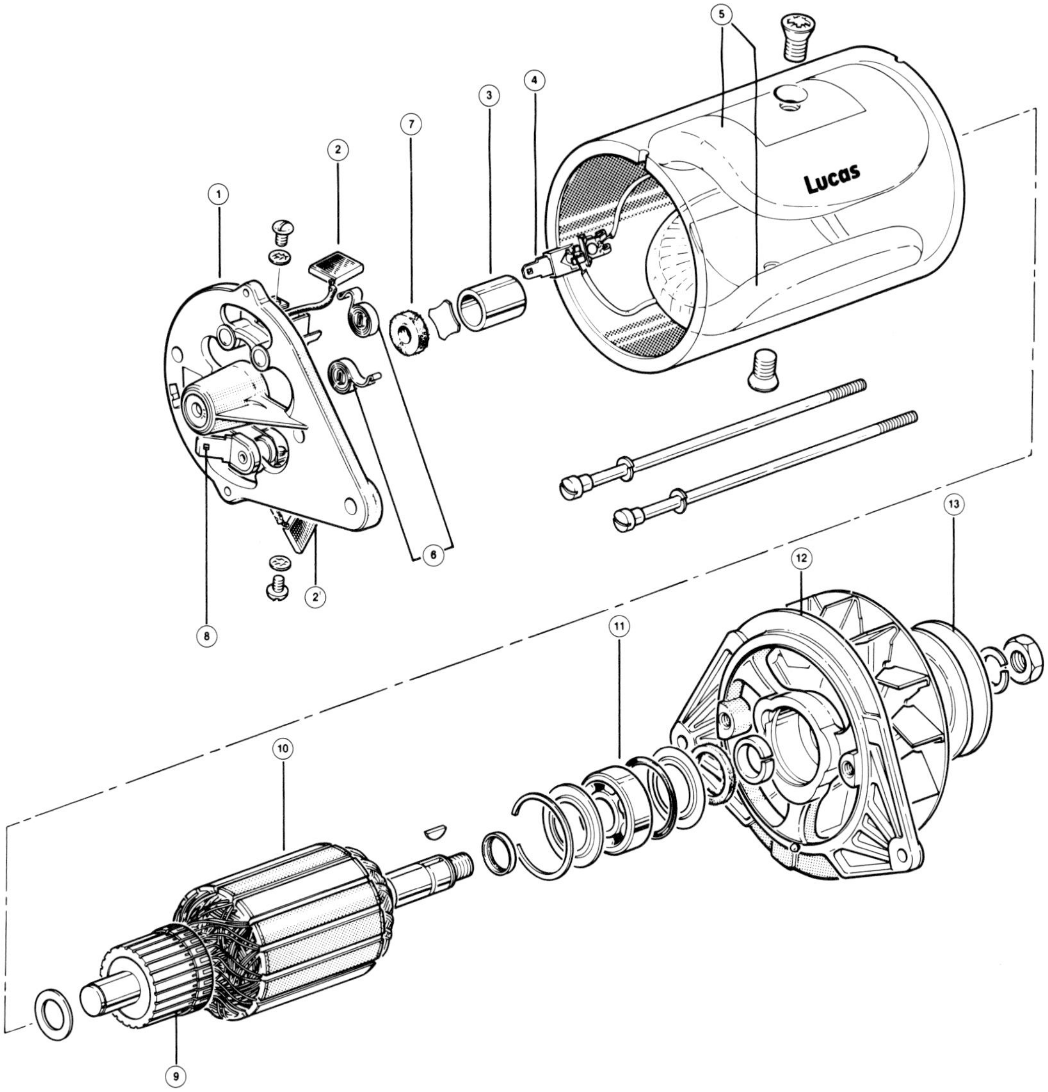

Fig 70. A typical dynamo.
1) Commutator end plate. 2) Brushes. 3) End plate. 4) Field coil terminal. 5) Field coils. 6) Brush springs. 7) Felt oil ring. 8) Output terminal. 9) Commutator. 10) Armature. 11) Drive end bearing. 12) Drive end plate. 13) Drive pulley.

come from elsewhere on the craft, e.g. external current voltage control regulators, propeller shafts, etc. The reader who has this problem is advised to contact a manufacturer such as Lucas Marine, who publish a useful guide in their booklet entitled *Marine Electrical Systems*, from which some of the information given here has been quoted.

Dynamos

These are sometimes still fitted to small marine engines and there are many engines in service with them. Their main disadvantage is their relatively low output at low engine speeds, but they will continue to give good service providing simple maintenance procedures are carried out. These are seeing that the commutator remains clean and free from pitting and scoring, and that the carbon brushes are not unduly worn and are free to slide in the brush boxes. Brush springs weakened by corrosion should be replaced. These should be checked after every 200–300 hours of service, and at the same time a little oil injected into the oil hole provided in the end brackets in some older models.

thirteen
Non-electric Starting

Alternative Methods

Over the years many attempts have been made to produce satisfactory alternatives to electrical means of starting small diesel engines. These have included the use of percussion type cartridges, wind-up inertia starters, hydraulic and compressed air motors and manual cranking by conveniently arranged raised cranking handles. Such methods have met with varying degrees of success, but it is only the latter which has enjoyed fairly widespread use in the smallest size of engine and which merits attention here.

Decompressors

Starting by any method depends on reaching a sufficiently high cranking speed, and in particular speed over the compression stroke. Engines intended to be hand started are usually equipped with a decompressor and a heavy flywheel so that, in conjunction with the momentum already given to the flywheel, an effort being applied to the crank handle will carry the piston over the point of maximum compression at top centre while the fuel is injected. The decompressor is usually a small lever on the valve rocker cover, and acts by preventing the exhaust valves from closing. A little practice is required in operating it at the right moment, while still maintaining hand cranking effort. Before trying to start an engine from cold, it is a good idea to turn the engine over several times with the decompressor in operation. This will do two things. The first is to break any stickiness in the cylinders and bearings, and the second is to prime the injectors with fuel so that an audible squeak as each piston approaches top dead centre indicates that injection is taking place.

Excess Fuel Devices

Some engines may be fitted with a device or lever on the fuel pump which permits an excess quantity of fuel to be delivered for starting. This should be set to operate before cranking. It will be automatically disengaged as soon as the engine runs and the governor takes charge. On no account should an excess fuel device be interfered with or an attempt made to fix it in an operative position during normal running.

Stopping

Likewise any decompression lever should be kept in the fully off or 'run' position whenever the engine is running, and the temptation to use it to stop the engine and so avoid the usual thump which occurs when most diesels are stopped, should be resisted. Stopping should always be carried out by using the

Fig 71. Solenoid operation of stop control on Watermota engine (Synchrostart).

spring loaded fuel pump 'stop' lever which cuts off fuel delivery, and it must be held until the engine comes to rest. A periodic examination of the latter should be made to ensure that any linkage is free and responds to the action of the return spring if fitted. Remember to ensure that the lever is set to 'run' position before attempting the next start.

fourteen
Tools

This chapter is not for those with expertise and training in the use of hand tools. On the other hand, not everyone connected with small diesels would claim to be an expert mechanic, and it is the latter class of reader for whom the following notes may not be amiss. Being an owner or skipper of a small craft requires some ability to be able to do every kind of job connected with it. At least that ability can be a great help in an emergency and in less pressing moments a great time, temper and cost saver.

Hand Tools

The first thing needed is a tool kit. A manufacturer's recommended kit may well consist of a set of open-ended spanners or wrenches, plus a pair of pliers and a screw-driver or two, and last, but not least, a hammer. Seldom do these kits include just that kind of tool which is today regarded as an essential complement to the tool kit of every self respecting repair man or even a DIY buff. I am referring of course to sets of ring spanners or box socket wrenches, and sets of sockets with a variety of extension handles, preferably including a ratchet drive wrench. For serious repair work a torque measuring wrench is essential, because most manufacturers quote the proper torque figures to be applied to the more important or critical fastenings in the engine.

All wrenches should be marked with the size of hexagon for which they are intended to be used, i.e. the head of the bolt or nut, and these will normally be either in inch or metric sizes. The inch sizes are usually marked with a figure followed by the letters A/F, e.g. ⅝A/F means that the tool is intended to fit a nut or bolt or setscrew *head* which measures ⅝ in across two of the opposite and parallel flats of the hexagon. This is entirely to do with *hexagons* and not to the actual threads which can be one of several types chosen to suit the purpose best. Likewise engines built with metric parts will require spanners marked in whole numbers (which represent the width across the flats of the nut or bolt head in millimetres).

Another tool which will sometimes be found useful is a soft-faced hammer, one side of the head of which is inserted with a soft metal and the other side with rawhide. This can be used on objects which would other-wise be damaged or bruised by a steel hammer. A hacksaw is desirable with a selection of spare blades, 24 teeth per inch is a good general purpose blade. An adjustable or crescent wrench is also an essential tool but, because of its versatility, it is often abused and used where a conventional tool would be equal or better. It should always be adjusted to fit the hexagon of any bolt or nut snugly, otherwise there is danger of it slipping and causing both damage to the user and damage to the hexagon.

Tools for Overhaul

When it comes to overhaul tasks, a number of

special tools are needed to facilitate certain of them. These tools will not be needed for the day-to-day tasks of caring for the engine and are not usually to be found in the tool kits of the average user. They are, however, important additions to his normal tool kit, to be considered if he contemplates carrying out anything more than a top overhaul. The first of these, already referred to in chapter Three, is, a piston ring expander, without which it can be difficult to remove rings from the piston without breaking them. The other tool needed is the piston ring compressor fixture, which is invaluable in inserting pistons complete with rings into the cylinders. A torque measuring wrench is invaluable if not an actual necessity, and there are various makes and types on the market which replace guesswork when doing up vital fastenings, such as connecting rod bolts and cylinder head nuts. These wrenches have either a dial mounted in the handle, or a friction adjustment which can be set to a pre-determined tension so that it is impossible to overtighten a nut.

Last but not least are the measuring devices which mechanics tend to take for granted, but which the average car or boat owner seldom carries around or keeps in his garage at home. These are the micrometers and dial gauges which are essential when everything has been dismantled, and you are having to decide what new parts are required to rebuild to reasonable standards.

About the only measuring devices which must be in the user's kit are a steel straightedge or rule and a set of thickness gauges known as 'feelers' (Fig 72). Whilst it requires considerable experience to be able to take an exact measurement with a thickness gauge or set of feelers, because accuracy depends to a large extent on the ability of the user to feel when there is correct tension on the blade, its use is essential in determining valve tappet to rocker clearances. Wear on one or other of these engine parts can make the measurement of the actual running clearance more difficult, because it may be uneven; see chapter Five.

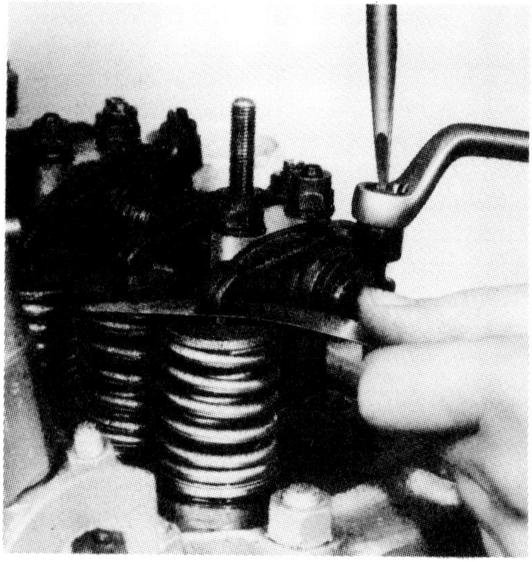

Fig 72. The use of feeler gauges to measure valve clearances.

A feeler gauge consists of a number of blades ground to an exact thickness that is marked on each blade, which can then be used separately or together until they form a snug fit between two surfaces (Fig 73). It will be noticed that the thin blades are protected by thicker blades each side or them; if thin blades are wanted they should be unfolded along with the thick blades as far as possible, to avoid damaging them. Care must be taken to prevent them becoming kinked or bent by being forced into spaces too small to accept them. If they are not required to be used often, they should be lightly oiled before they are put away and then wiped clean and dry before they are next used. It is surprising how they become rusty when kept in a tool box on board a boat – and then become useless.

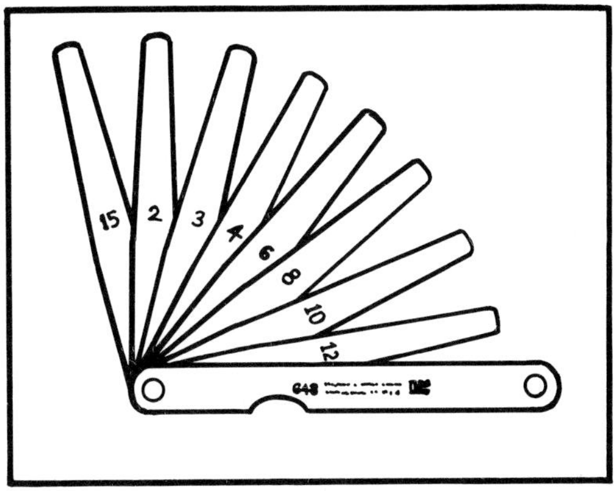

Fig 73. Thickness Gauges – *The most indispensable gauge used by the engine mechanic is a thickness gauge, such as illustrated. It will be seen that this tool, which is often called a 'feeler' gauge, consists of a number of blades that can be folded into a hollow handle. Each of the blades is accurately ground to an exact thickness, which is marked in thousandths of an inch on the blade. To use this tool various blades or combinations of blades are inserted between the two surfaces until a snug fit is obtained.*

Special Tools

Special tools for a particular model of engine are usually costly because they are made in relatively small numbers by specialists. They fall outside the scope of the occasional user but are invaluable for the overhaul of a number of units. The boat owner can afford to ignore them for all practical purposes, unless he is a commercial user with a fleet of several craft to maintain himself. The overhaul of a number of items mentioned in the foregoing chapters, e.g. electrical equipment such as alternators, merits the attention of specialists. Injectors and fuel pumps fall within this category, because they can only be set or calibrated by means of equipment outside the scope of the average engine user. A hand injector tester is an invaluable, if not essential, tool for a multi-boat operator, but a fuel pump bench would hardly be justified. Ammeters, voltmeters and test lamps are essential tools for any boat-yard or marina electrician.

Other test equipment for diesels made today include compression testers and engine analysers, all designed to help ensure that the

Fig 74. An atomizer tester (TI Dieseltune).

efficiency of installed engines can readily be checked and maintained. Compression testers, which are basically pressure gauges fitted in turn in the hole in each cylinder normally occupied by the injection nozzle to measure the maximum pressure, are simple enough devices, but the readings obtained are of comparative value only. The pressure reading in each cylinder is obtained while the engine is cranked by the starter motor (and considerable variations can be measured, dependent on cranking speed) and in any case is not directly related to the theoretical pressure obtainable with that particular engine. As diagnostic tools, therefore, such devices have somewhat limited value, and depend entirely on the ability of the user to interpret the results obtained. They may show up one or more cylinders to be lacking in compression and therefore in need of further investigation, but the actual values read on the gauge are not of particular significance. Some makers suggest running the engine at idling speed, the actual speed being controlled by the engine throttle so that it is always the same as each cylinder is tested in turn, in order to secure more strictly comparable results. Engine makers may publish figures which can be used for comparative purposes. Small single or twin cylinder engines which have a hand cranking handle are best assessed for condition by using this means alone, i.e. the handle.

Portable electronic equipment is available on the market which can enable injection timing to be assessed while the engine is running. Its use involves disconnecting the injection pipe to one of the cylinders and inserting, between the injector and the normal union connector at the end of the pipe, a transducer which responds to the fuel pressure in the pipe and thus the moment of commencement of lift of the injector needle. This response is electrically conveyed to a hand held instrument about the size of a pocket calculator, where the number of degrees in advance of top dead centre at which injection is taking place can be read off from a digital display. This equipment, known as the 241 Digital Engine Analyser, can be of help to the specialist repair man who has knowledge of what the dynamic timing of the engine should be at any point of the speed range.

appendix A
Fuels and Lubricants

Fuels

While the diesel will run on a wide variety of liquid fuel, it is not insensitive to variations in fuel quality and it behoves the user to obtain his supplies from a reputable source, if satisfaction is to be obtained in terms of performance and life of the engine. Official specifications for light diesel fuel or gas oil are recognised internationally under one or more of the following descriptions:

Germany – DIN.51601
UK – BS2869–A1/A2
USA – ASTMD.975–2D

Fuel to any one of the above should be satisfactory for high speed marine diesels, but it is as well to bear in mind the constant need for cleanliness in handling and storage.

Lubricants

Typical specifications of suitable engine oils are given as follows, and oils may usually be found throughout the world which correspond to at least one of these:

American Petroleum Institute (API) – for service designation DG or DG/DM.
Complying with US Military specification MIL–L–2104C or MIL–L–45199B.
Complying with UK Defence specification DEF.2104C.

appendix B Some Do's and Don't's

Keep engine clean.	It is much easier to work on and find faults or leaks. It will not smell of fuel if there is no trace of fuel around.
Keep exhaust clean.	There is no need for black smoke.
Keep bilges clean.	Use bilge cleaner or washing-up fluid (in moderation) to keep it free from grease and smell. Be careful where you dump bilge water, especially in inland waterways.

Check external nuts and bolts for tightness periodically.

Always make sure the 'stop' control on the fuel pump is inoperative before attempting to start the engine.

Make sure cooling water is being discharged overboard after starting up. Check intake strainers.

Never allow the engine to overheat, investigate immediately.

Keep water pump and generator belts correctly tensioned, with a spare belt on board.

Do not use decompressors for stopping the engine except in emergency.

Do not stop engine in gear. Hydraulically operated gears may not automatically return to neutral, thus impairing restarting.

Do service fuel and lube oil filters regularly.

Do check oil level and pressure regularly.

Do check engine mounting bolts periodically.

Do check prop shaft coupling bolts periodically.

Do get to use hand tools regularly, so that you know which spanner or wrench is the correct one for a particular nut.

Always use clean fuel, and never let the fuel tank run dry even when the boat is heeled.

Don't attempt to tune the engine by altering the injection pump timing, injector setting pressure, pump fuel setting, from maker's original setting.

Do remember to check every season zinc anti-corrosion pencils or other devices, if fitted by makers, to combat electrolytic corrosion.

appendix C
Some Useful Conversions

To convert from	*to*	*Multiply by*
Brake horsepower	Watts	746.0
Cubic centimetres	Cubic inches	0.061
Cubic inches	Cubic centimetres	16.39
Cubic metres	Cubic feet	35.31
Gallons	Litres	4.543
Gallons	US gallons	1.2
Horsepower (UK)	Metric horsepower	1.014
Inches	Metres	0.0254
Inches	Millimetres	25.4
Kilograms	Pounds	2.205
Kg/sq cm	p.s.i.	14.22
Kg/sq metre	Pounds/square foot	0.205
Litres	Cubic inches	61.0
Litres	Gallons	0.22
Litres	Pints	1.761
Metres	Feet	3.28
Metres	Inches	39.37
Metric horsepower	Horsepower	0.986
Metric horsepower	Kilowatts	0.735
Millimetres	Inches	0.039
Pints	Litres	0.5689
Pounds	Kilograms	0.4536
lb/bhp/hr	Grams/cheval/heure	447.4
psi	Kg/sq cm	0.0703
Short tons (USA)	Tons	0.893
Square inches	Square millimetres	645.16
US gallons	Gallons (Imperial)	0.833

Horsepower

Although we are accustomed to talk about horsepower as a measure of power developed by an engine it is by no means a precise definition. First of all the term means something different in many countries which may have different languages, e.g. Germany, France, Britain and the USA, and each country has different conditions of test laid down in order to make the necessary measurements of power. In order to achieve some degree of commonality there has been over recent years a movement in Europe to adopt the SI system in engineering measurements, and the relationship of the most important of these is given opposite.

Ratio of the International System of Units (SI), the Metric System, and British Units

	SI Units	Metric Units	British Units
Force	N (Newton)	kgf (kilogram-force)	lbf (poundforce)
	1	0.1019716	0.2248
	9.80665	1	2.2
	4.44822	0.4536	1
Torque	Nm (Newtonmeter)	kgmf (kilogram-forcemeter)	ft.lbs (footpounds)
	1	0.1019716	0.7376
	9.80665	1	7.2330
	1.3558	0.1383	1
Pressure kPa	(kiloPascal)	kgf/cm^2	psi (lbs/sq inch)
	1	0.01020	0.14508
	98.0665	1	14.2233
	6.8941	0.0703	1
Power	KW (kiloWatt)	HP (Horsepower)	BHP (brake horsepower)
	1	1.36	1.34
	0.735	1	0.986
	0.745	1.014	1
Heat	kJ (kiloJoules)	kcal (kilocalories)	BTU (British Thermal Units)
	1	0.239	0.9484
	4.1868	1	3.968
	1.0544	0.252	1

Note 1. kilo = 1000
2. 1 N/m^2 = 1 Pa

appendix D
Fault Diagnosis

Fault Finding Chart

Fault	Possible Cause
Low cranking speed	1, 2, 3, 4.
Will not start	5, 6, 7, 8, 9, 10, 12, 13, 14, 15, 16, 17, 18, 19, 20, 22, 31, 32, 33.
Difficult starting	5, 7, 8, 9, 10, 11, 12, 13, 14, 15, 16, 18, 19, 20, 21, 22, 24, 29, 31, 32, 33.
Lack of power	8, 9, 10, 11, 12, 13, 14, 18, 19, 20, 21, 22, 23, 24, 25, 26, 27, 31, 32, 33, 60, 62, 63.
Misfiring	8, 9, 10, 12, 13, 14, 16, 18, 19, 20, 25, 26, 28, 29, 30, 32.
Excessive fuel consumption	11, 13, 14, 16, 18, 19, 20, 22, 23, 24, 25, 27, 28, 29, 31, 32, 33, 62, 63.
Black exhaust	11, 13, 14, 16, 18, 19, 20, 22, 24, 25, 27, 28, 29, 31, 32, 33, 60, 63.
Blue/White exhaust	4, 16, 18, 19, 20, 25, 27, 31, 33, 34, 35, 45, 56, 61.
Low oil pressure	4, 36, 37, 38, 39, 40, 42, 43, 44, 53, 58.
Knocking	9, 14, 16, 18, 19, 22, 26, 28, 29, 31, 33, 35, 36, 45, 46, 59.
Erratic running	7, 8, 9, 10, 11, 12, 13, 14, 16, 20, 21, 23, 26, 28, 29, 30, 33, 35, 45, 59.
Vibration	13, 14, 20, 23, 25, 26, 29, 30, 33, 45, 48, 49.
High oil pressure	4, 38, 41.
Overheating	11, 13, 14, 16, 18, 19, 24, 25, 45, 47, 50, 51, 52, 53, 54, 57.
Excessive crankcase pressure	25, 31, 33, 34, 45, 55.
Poor compression	11, 19, 25, 28, 29, 31, 32, 33, 34, 46, 59.

Key to Fault Finding Chart

1. *Battery capacity low.*
2. *Bad electrical connections.*
3. *Faulty starter motor.*
4. *Incorrect grade of lubricating oil.*
5. *Low cranking speed.*
6. *Fuel tank empty.*
7. *Faulty stop control operation.*
8. *Blocked fuel feed pipe.*
9. *Faulty fuel lift pump.*
10. *Choked fuel filter.*
11. *Restriction in air cleaner or induction system.*
12. *Air in fuel system.*
13. *Faulty fuel injection pump.*
14. *Faulty atomisers or incorrect type.*
15. *Incorrect use of cold start equipment.*
16. *Faulty cold starting equipment.*
17. *Broken fuel injection pump drive.*
18. *Incorrect fuel pump timing.*
19. *Incorrect valve timing.*
20. *Poor compression.*
21. *Blocked fuel tank vent.*
22. *Incorrect type or grade of fuel.*
23. *Sticking throttle or restricted movement.*
24. *Exhaust pipe restriction.*
25. *Cylinder head gasket leaking.*
26. *Overheating.*
27. *Cold running.*
28. *Incorrect tappet adjustment.*
29. *Sticking valves.*
30. *Incorrect high pressure pipes.*
31. *Worn cylinder bores.*
32. *Pitted valves and seats.*
33. *Broken, worn or sticking piston ring(s).*
34. *Worn valve stems and guides.*
35. *Overfull air cleaner or use of incorrect grade of oil.*
36. *Worn or damaged bearings.*
37. *Insufficient oil in sump.*
38. *Inaccurate gauge.*
39. *Oil pump worn.*
40. *Pressure relief valve sticking open.*
41. *Pressure relief valve sticking closed.*
42. *Broken relief valve spring.*
43. *Faulty suction pipe.*
44. *Choked oil filter.*
45. *Piston seizure/pick up.*
46. *Incorrect piston height.*
47. *Sea cock strainer or heat exchanger blocked.*
48. *Faulty engine mounting (housing).*
49. *Incorrectly aligned flywheel housing or flywheel.*
50. *Faulty thermostat.*
51. *Restriction in water jacket.*
52. *Loose water pump drive belt.*
53. *Gearbox or engine oil cooler choked.*
54. *Faulty water pump.*
55. *Choked breather pipe.*
56. *Damaged valve stem oil deflectors (if fitted).*
57. *Coolant level too low.*
58. *Blocked sump strainer.*
59. *Broken valve spring.*
60. *Damaged or dirty turbocharger impeller.*
61. *Leaking turbocharger oil seals.*
62. *Leaking induction system (turbocharged engines only).*
63. *Plastic bag fouling propellor, or weed etc on bottom.*

appendix E
Laying-up for the Winter

Most manufacturers recommend procedures to be applied where engines are laid up for periods. At the risk of seeming to give contrary advice I would suggest that these procedures are sometimes unnecessarily complicated or elaborate. So much depends on the length of time the engine is actually out of use and the degree of adverse climatic conditions which are experienced. I prefer to run my engine once a month for about 15 minutes with antifreeze in the indirect cooling system, the boat remaining in the water meanwhile. In the UK where, in contrast with North America and Scandinavia, the winters are not very severe, the need for special wax-free fuel to be run through the system is not so important, provided of course that you don't want actually to start the engine under extreme winter conditions. A small incidence of overnight frost will not necessarily crack cylinder castings, blow out core plugs, or damage water pump impellers, but these are the points which the owner must be worried about if he has failed to drain all untreated coolant from the system. He should get to know all the lowest points from which coolant remaining in the system can be drained, and make sure nothing remains by slackening hose clips and water pump covers if need be. Remember the high cost and inconvenience of replacing a cracked cylinder head or block justifies the seemingly over-careful owner. This is the advice of one well-known manufacturer to those owners laying up their engines for a period of several months:

1. Replace fuel in tank with a small supply of calibration fluid or equivalent.

2. Drain lubricating oil from sump and refill with Shell Ensis 20 or equivalent.

3. Run the engine for a period to circulate the Ensis oil through the system and to ensure the calibration fluid is passed through the fuel pump and injectors.

4. Stop the engine and drain off the Ensis lubricating oil from the sump, after which the crankshaft should NOT be turned until the engine is again required for service. The calibration fluid should be left in the fuel system.

5. Drain all water from the engine.

6. Seal all openings on the engine with tape.

7. Remove batteries and store fully charged with the terminals coated with vaseline (petroleum jelly).

8. Grease all external bright parts and control linkages, etc.

9. Tie labels on the engine clearly stating what steps have been taken to inhibit the engine during storage, as above.

If the above is not carried out then the engine should be run about 15 minutes once a month – preferably on load.

Index